Natural History Rambles:
Western Peak District

David Mycroft

Published by Sigma Leisure – an imprint of
Sigma Press, 1 South Oak Lane, Wilmslow, Cheshire SK9 6AR, England.

Whilst every effort has been made to ensure that the information given in this book is correct, neither the publisher nor the author accept any responsibility for any inaccuracy.

British Library Cataloguing in Publication Data
A CIP record for this book is available from the British Library.

ISBN: 1-85058-280-7

Typesetting and Design by: Sigma Press, Wilmslow, Cheshire

Illustrations by: Martin Mills

Cover design: Martin Mills

Maps by: Pam Upchurch

Printed by: The Cromwell Press, Melksham, Wiltshire

Acknowledgements: The author wishes to thank Stuart Poynton, Terry Owen, Lisa Gilham, and Jan and Geoff Cole for assistance with research for this book. Special thanks are also due to Dr. Alan (Fergie) Morrison for valuable advice.

Contents

Buxton and the Goyt Valley 49

The Manifold and Dove Valleys 89

The Peak District – an Introduction to its Natural History

In the forty years since its designation as Britain's first national park the Peak District has become increasingly popular with ramblers for its wide open spaces and easy access. In recent years the number of visitors it attracts annually has placed it second behind Mt. Fujiyama in the world's most visited national parks. Some 4000 miles of public footpaths criss-cross the area giving a wide variety of walks, from the peat moorlands of Kinder Scout and Bleaklow to the secluded dales of the Manifold and Lathkill.

Open Moors and Large Caves

To the north and west of the park lies the Dark Peak, where sharp gritstone edges and high moorlands dominate. Here you can walk over open moors through mile after mile of heather and bracken. A wide variety of long distance pathways has been created to tempt the serious walker, including the Pennine Way which winds along the Pennines from Edale to Kirk Yetholm in the Scottish borders.

The central and southern parts of the Peak are of a different nature entirely, lying on the older more porous limestones. In the White Peak rivers have cut deep valleys in a plateau before disappearing underground into large cave systems. It is also an area full of the scars of two thousand years of continuous exploitation for natural resources.

This diversity of topography has led to a wide variety of natural habitats, and the region is home to an outstanding number of bird and plant species. With the range of acid moorlands, river valleys, deciduous and coniferous plantations and open reservoirs it is possible to view a wide diversity of wildlife, both local and migratory, in a single day's walking.

Ancient Packhorse Routes

The area covered by this book lies partly within, and partly outside the boundaries of the national park, and contains parts of three counties. At Three Shires Head, a popular spot for walkers, the old packhorse routes meet at a junction of Derbyshire, Staffordshire and Cheshire over the River Dane. With luck it is also possible to see as far as the Welsh hills from several spots in the area, in addition to a further four or five counties. Over 20 million people live within a fifty mile radius of the Peak Park, and with Buxton, England's highest market town, at the centre, the western Peak is easily accessible by public or private transport.

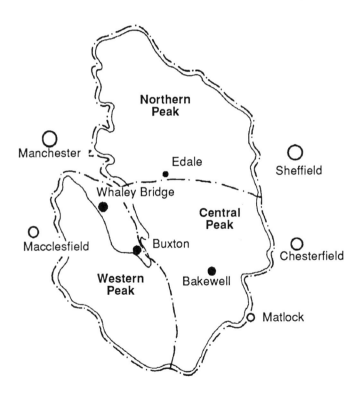

The Peak District and surrounding towns

The western region may be divided up for the purposes of this book into three distinct areas: Whaley Bridge, Buxton and the Goyt Valley, and the Manifold and Dove Valleys. Each of these areas has its own character and its own individual attractions both in terms of walking and natural history.

Natural History

The two most important factors influencing the natural history of an area are the underlying geology and human intervention. The western Peak is widely called a natural landscape, but is, in fact, more a result of man than of nature. While the geology is responsible for the soils, and therefore the life it can support, great changes have been made to both

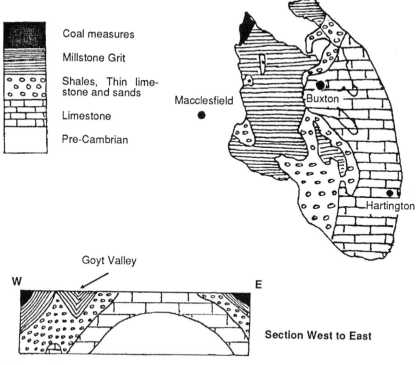

Coal measures

Millstone Grit

Shales, Thin lime-
stone and sands

Limestone

Pre-Cambrian

Macclesfield

Buxton

Hartington

Goyt Valley

W   E

Section West to East

Geology of the Western Peak

the soils and the distribution of water. As a result it is 5000 years of continuous habitation, climate and geology which determine the flora and fauna of the western Peak.

Geology

The Peak District is largely composed of a series of limestones and gritstones, interspersed with shales and thin sandstones, laid down 280 million years ago. The area was once covered in a series of younger limestones, sands and chalk, but a combination of folding, uplifting and erosion has removed the upper layers, leaving the carboniferous series exposed at the surface. The folding has resulted in a large dome called the Derbyshire Dome, with the older limestone exposed at the centre and the sands and grits exposed along the flanks.

Limestone

The limestones of the western Peak are a series of mainly massive, thick bedded strata of extremely high purity. They have given rise to an elevated plateau intersected by deep wood-lined dales. In its natural state the limestone created acid heaths as the natural habitat, but little of this still remains and it is now only in the deep valley sides that the native flora and fauna may be observed.

Millstone Grit

The shales and grits of the late carboniferous period form a horseshoe to the north, west and east of the limestone plateau. They are typified by high moorland and sharp escarpments. Bare rock is much more evident than in the limestone region, forming boundaries for the heather moors. Along the northern section of this horseshoe the Kinderscout Grit Group attains a maximum thickness of 1500 feet and is characterised by the thick bedded, coarse, pebbly gritstones associated with the edges commonly used for rock climbing.

Flora and Fauna

There are two distinct types of scenery in the western Peak, the White Peak of the Manifold and Dove Valleys and the Dark Peak of the western moors. These areas take their names from the underlying geology and from their general view. As the region is at the southern end of the Pennine Chain it benefits from some of southern England's advantages, while still retaining some of the attributes associated with high terrain and harsh climate. The result is that many species associated with the northern counties are still in evidence along with those associated with more southerly regions.

Originally the whole area was covered by trees, and evidence of this still remains in place names like Peak Forest, but man's intervention over the last 5000 years has altered the state of the countryside dramatically. The largest alterations started around the twelfth century in the White Peak when woodland destruction increased rapidly to make room for pastoral and arable land, while providing valuable timber for settlements and for use in lead smelting.

In the Dark Peak, peat had been building up for around 7000 years on the high moorland by the continuous decay of plant life under wet conditions. In places the peat even engulfed sections of the forest, as may be seen by stumps buried deep within it. The introduction of sheep, which was only possible with the building of permanent settlements, totally changed the balance. The sheep were grazed on the upper levels in summer and this grazing appears to have been a major influence on the halting of new peat formation by removing the surplus vegetation essential for new peat to build up. The removal of this surplus also exposed the upper layers of the peat to wind, causing desiccation. The problem has been further exacerbated by industrial pollution since the 19th century, carried from the nearby conurbations of Manchester. The latest in this line of destructive influences has been that of over-popularity. In places the peat has been eroded simply by the number of visitors walking over it.

White Peak

Before the influence of human beings much of the White Peak was covered in acid heath and woodland. The soils of the limestone plateau are free draining and lime and nutrients are easily leached resulting in high levels of acidity. In these conditions heather, bilberry and heath grasses flourish, along with yellow mountain pansy. Most of these heaths have been destroyed, however, in the course of continuous improvement for agriculture. The grassland which has replaced it is still abundant in plant life however, and it is easy to find thyme, blue scabious, lady's mantle, harebell, rockrose, purging flax, blue milkwort, orchids, meadow rue and violets.

The natural woodland of the White Peak is mainly ash and elm, with small leaved lime and yew as subsidiary species. Hazel and dogwood are also common in the few unaltered areas, but are replaced in many dales by lily-of-the-valley, bloody crane'sbill, dark red helleborine, spring cinquefoil and thistle, particularly in the steep valley sides.

Dark Peak

The high moors and peat bogs contain relatively few plant species in comparison with the species-rich limestone plateau. Heather and bilberry dominate large expanses along with cotton-grass. Sphagnum moss, formerly the dominant species, is now relatively scarce and associated with damp, dark, secluded spots in the moorland such as springs and hollows, in association with bog asphodel and cranberry. Other species include cowberry, bearberry, cloudberry and lesser twayblade.

Perhaps the most common, and easily recognisable, characteristic of the Dark Peak is the grouse moor. Here the heather is strictly controlled and managed for the purpose of rearing game birds. Grouse require a combination of young heather shoots for food and older heather for shelter and nesting. To provide this combination of old and young the gamekeeper undertakes a system of periodic burning to remove old heather and promote new growth. The result is a mosaic pattern clearly visible from the ground or the air.

The drier edges of the gritstone horseshoe exhibit remnants of the older native woodland, comprised mainly of sessile oak and silver birch, with occasional rowan and wych elm. Bluebell, bilberry bracken and rushes are also common, along with a variety of grasses such as sheep's fescue which is highly adapted to the acid soils and harsh climate.

Birds

The western Peak plays host to a wide number of bird species, both native and migratory. The two most characteristic birds are the ring ouzel and the red grouse. The ring ouzel is widely distributed throughout the British uplands, being spread throughout Scotland, north and central Wales, the south-western moors of Dartmoor, Bodmin Moor and Exmoor, along with the Pennines, and along with the meadow pipit is likely to be the most commonly sighted bird in the area. The red grouse, as mentioned previously, is a common sight on the managed heather moors, and has almost totally displaced its close relative the black grouse. Also common on the moorlands are the curlew, with its distinctive call, and the golden plover. In the wooded areas a wide variety of species are found including redstart, pied flycatcher, and wood warblers.

The open waters of Errwood and Fernilee Reservoirs, along with the rivers flowing off Axe Edge provide habitats for heron, kingfisher, wheatear, dipper and a variety of native and migratory ducks. Also common throughout the park is the odd-looking crossbill (see page 22)

Dipper (top) and Mallard

Animals

There are very few native animals left in the Peak Park, the majority having been lost through 5000 years of human occupation. Changes in agriculture have been responsible for the demise of certain species, while introducing foreign species has led to a decrease in number of others.

Of the native species the most noticeable is the local Derbyshire gritstone sheep, especially suited to survival in rough moorland under harsh conditions. They have even been known to survive for weeks on the moors when snow has cut off the local settlements preventing the farmers from reaching them. They are immediately discernible from other sheep by their black and white patched faces. Two local species of animal show seasonal adaptations which aid in their identification. The stoat is rare due to the attentions of farmers, but may be spotted in some of the secluded limestone dales. It is easily distinguished from the weasel by its larger size (35-40cm compared to 20-25cm) and the black tip on the tail in summer. In winter it may turn almost completely white, but is more commonly grey. The weasel is also native to the area, living on rats, mice voles and small rabbits.

The mountain hare is a common sight on the moorlands of the Peak, and to a lesser extent in the limestone valleys. It differs from the common brown hare by its smaller size (50-65cm compared to 60-70cm) and shorter ears. The fur is commonly blue-grey, though it may turn white in winter. The red squirrel may also be seen occasionally in certain locations, but is more commonly replaced by the grey squirrel which is better adapted to ground foraging. Apart from the obvious difference in colour the red squirrel is smaller (28-40cm) than the grey (45-50cm), and is rarely seen on the ground.

Trees

As mentioned above, the native trees of the western Peak are the ash, elm, rowan, yew, hawthorn, beech, alder and birch. The Scots pine, Britain's only native pine tree is also indigenous to the area, but is commonly replaced with European and Japanese larch and sitka spruce. These alien conifers have been introduced for plantations due to their increased productivity. In areas of mixed and coniferous woodland the easiest way to identify individual trees is by either leaf shape in the case of deciduous trees or cone shape for evergreens.

Alder
The alder is more common in marshy places and beside streams. The leaves are rounded with an indented tip. Catkins are born on old wood, with male and female easily distinguished. The male catkins are purple with yellow flowers, the female are small and purple-brown. When

mature the female catkins grow into a hard, brown, false cone.

Ash

The ash tree has a neat crown when young which soon dies back as the tree matures to become ragged. The twigs are grey with large, black buds, and pinnate leaves. The leaves are thin, short-stalked, toothed ovals with 3-7 pairs of leaflets to each leaf. The ash is one of the commonest native species in Britain, and is particularly associated with limestone soils.

Beech

The beech is a spreading tree forming natural woodlands on well drained dry soils. The bark is smooth and grey, and its oval leaves are veined and silky. Male flowers are found in clusters hanging down on long stalks; female flowers are smaller and more upright. The common beech nuts are, in fact, the ripened female flowers.

Birch

Birch is a rapid spreading pioneer tree, which colonises new ground. Once its seeds are established it grows rapidly but tends to have a relatively short life. The branches droop at the tips and display shiny twigs. Leaf shape is a pointed oval with long and short teeth. In April and May it is conspicuous due to the male catkins drooping from it.

Elm

The common elm of the Peak is the wych elm which is much more resistant to Dutch elm disease than the English elm. The wych elm has a spreading crown similar to that of the oak, and a similar rough bark. The major, obvious, difference is in the leaf shape. The elm leaf is very short stalked and rough. The leaf shape is a broad, toothed oval, commonly divided unevenly.

Oak

The durmast oak is the native variety of oak, but most of it has been replaced by hybrids. The pedunculate oak is very familiar with a broad crown, heavily ridged bark and bent branches. The leaves are deeply lobed on small stalks. The acorns of the pedunculate oak are on a long stalked cup. The durmast oak differs from the pedunculate by having a longer stalked leaf, stalkless acorns and a more tapered leaf base.

Rowan
The rowan is commonly referred to as the mountain ash, and is similar in many ways. It is common as a single individual on ridges and hilltops throughout the area. The leaf shape is similar to that of the ash, with a pinnate leaf and several pairs of leaflets. The rowan is, however, easily distinguished from the ash by its size and shape. The rowan is more slender than the ash and its branches rise steeply, as opposed to those of the ash which are more radiant.

Yew
The yew is an extremely long living tree commonly associated with churchyards throughout the country. In the western peak it is associated with steep-sided limestone dales. The bark is flaking and red in colour, based on a buttressed trunk. The leaves appear as long, thin, flattened needles, dark green in colour.

Conifers

The wet peaty hills of the western Peak are particularly suitable for large scale growing of conifers in plantations. These are a common sight around the edges of reservoirs and on steep valley sides where the ground is unsuitable for other plants or trees. By far the easiest way of distinguishing between species is to examine the cone size and shape.

Larch
There are two pure species of larch, the European and the Japanese, which together have produced a fast-growing, productive hybrid, larix eurolepsis. The larch has grey-brown, fissured bark and limp bright green needles growing in rosettes. The female cone is initially purple, but hardens to a small, smooth, egg-shaped cone, on the European larch. On the Japanese larch the female cone has out-turned scales. The hybrid is between the two, and is becoming increasingly common.

Scots Pine
The Scots pine is the only conifer native to Britain which is still commercially planted. It is distinguishable by its orange-brown trunk and branches. The needles are in pairs with male ones clustering around the shoot tips in spring. It also differs from other common pines in its usual habit of growing more on one side than the other, and its limited number of branches except at the upper levels of the trunk. The female cone is small and matures from green to a grey-brown colour.

Sitka Spruce and cone

Sitka Spruce

The sitka spruce is perhaps the most common plantation conifer in Britain. It has short, sharp, flattened, bluish needles which grow on "pegs", which remain when the needles fall to leave rough twigs. The cone is much more elongated and cylindrical than those of the pine or larch, making it readily identifiable.

Seeds

The other way of identifying conifers is by studying the seed shape.

Seeds are located in pairs behind the scales of the cone, and have papery wings which vary in outline in each species. The Japanese larch wing is semi-circular with the seed protruding from the straight edged corner of the semi-circle. The sitka spruce wing is more elongated, forming an oval with the seed filling one end. The wing of the Scots pine is larger than the other two species and is spatulate in shape.

Walking In the Western Peak

The hills and moors of the western Peak are a beautiful area for walking, but may also be a very dangerous place. When walking in the area please ensure you go properly equipped, with warm clothing, strong walking boots, waterproofs and a map and compass.

Although maps of each walk are included in this book they are meant as an outline guide and are no substitute for an Ordnance Survey map. The White Peak and Dark Peak maps at 2.5 inches to the mile cover almost all the walks in this area and are a very good investment. It is also important to learn the techniques of route finding by map and compass, the weather in the western Peak is very changeable and can close in within a matter of minutes.

When walking in the peak please observe the Country Code, and try to leave the countryside as you found it for the enjoyment of others.

Leave no litter
Keep to footpaths
Protect wildlife, plants and trees
Fasten all gates
Keep off walls, fences and hedges
Safeguard all water supplies
Guard against risk of fire
Keep dogs under control
Respect the life of the country
Go carefully on roads

When undertaking a strenuous or long distance walk it is always advisable to leave a description of your route, and an expected time of return with someone responsible. Please ensure that you inform them on your return to avoid search parties looking for you unnecessarily.

Places of interest

Buxton
England's second highest market town, at the heart of the western Peak. Attractions include Georgian Architecture, Roman spa baths, Poole's Cavern, Opera House, Pavillion Gardens, Country Park and Micrarium.

Cat & Fiddle Inn
England's second highest licenced pub standing high on the moors above Buxton, giving access to the Goyt Valley and Axe Edge Moor.

The Chestnut Centre
An owl and otter sanctuary between Chapel-en-le-Frith and Castleton. Open to the public for a small charge, the centre includes breeding pens and a nature walk through deciduous woodland.

Cromford and High Peak Railway
Remains exist throughout the Whaley Bridge and Buxton areas. Built in 1830 to link the Peak Forest Canal and Cromford Canal, passenger services ceased in 1877 after a fatality. Inclines may still be seen at Whaley Bridge and Bunsal Cob (Goyt Valley).

Eccles Pike
A National Trust property with fine views over Chapel-en- le-Frith and the surrounding district.

Ecton Hill
During the 18th century this was the site of Europe's most productive copper mines, and many remains are still visible.

Errwood Hall
Built in 1830 by the Grimshawe family in the heart of the Goyt Valley. The hall is now a ruin on the west side of Errwood Reservoir, but the grounds still contain a large variety of flora.

Flash
England's highest village, on the A53 south of Buxton.

Hartington

Gateway to the upper Dove Valley. Attractions include Hartington Hall and a world famous cheese factory.

Ilam

Gateway to the lower Dove and Manifold valleys. Attractions include Ilam Hall, Country Park, Izaak Walton Hotel, Gothic Cross, church with Saxon remains and large sculpture by Sir Francis Chantrey.

Ilam Hall (by permission, Peak National Park)

Longnor

Rejuvenated village with good access to both the Dove and Manifold valleys. During the 1980s the village was part of an E.E.C. experiment in rural culture.

Tissington

The annual well dressing on Ascension Day is traditionally the first of the year.

Wildboarclough
A small village to the west of the area, most famous for its clear spring waters which are now bottled and sold nationwide.

Wild Boar Inn
A public house on the Buxton to Congleton road, of interest for its wild boar skin wearing glasses.

Windgather Rocks
A popular rock climbing centre in the Vale of Kettleshulme.

A traditional well dressing

Area covered in this book

O HAYFIELD

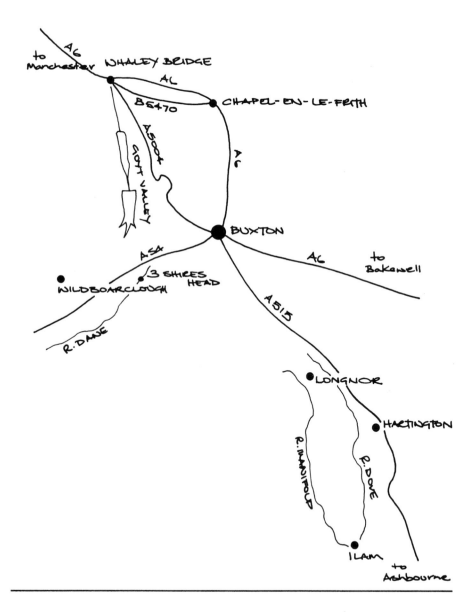

The Walks

Details of bus and train services given are correct as this book goes to press, but are subject to change. Please check with the bus companies and British Rail before setting out. The following contacts may be helpful:

Tourist Information Centres

Buxton: (0298) 25106
Chesterfield: (0246) 207777
Macclesfield: (0625) 500500
Manchester: 061-456-4195
Matlock: (0629) 55082
Sheffield: (0742) 734671

Bus Services

Cheshire
General: (0625) 534850
C-Line Bus Co. (Macclesfield): (0625) 617222

Derbyshire
Buxton area: (0298) 23098
Chesterfield area: (0246) 250450 and (0246) 207103
Derby area: (0332) 292200

Greater Manchester
GM Buses: 061-273-5341

Bus and Train information can be obtained from Greater Manchester Passenger Transport Executive on 061-228-7811 (useful network map available)

Train Services
BR inquiries: 061 832 8353

Foreground: cross-leaved heather; behind the pool is Tormentil (enlarged for clarity) with a traditional dry-stone wall as a backdrop.

Whaley Bridge

To the north west of the Peak Park the villages of Whaley Bridge, Chapel-en-le-Frith and Chinley lie only ten miles from Stockport and the edge of Greater Manchester. Access is via the A6 Manchester to Derby road, or train from Manchester Piccadilly. Of the three villages Whaley Bridge is the most convenient for walkers, lying midway between Buxton and Stockport.

The village of Whaley Bridge makes interesting walking in its own right, having a distinguished history. The village grew up along an arm of the Peak Forest Canal and the main road between Matlock and Manchester, later to become the A6. In 1830 the Cromford and High Peak Railway was opened to connect the canal with that and Cromford near Matlock, for transporting limestone from nearby quarries, and milk for the big cities. The line has long since closed, though a horse incline is still visible near the canal wharf, and the canal is only used by pleasure craft. In recent years even the A6 has been diverted, though the railway line still remains.

To the west of Whaley Bridge lie the last hills of the peak. The walking is varied in nature from low level rambles around Toddbrook Reservoir to the last of the gritstone edges before the monotony of the Cheshire Plain. It is similar to the area around the Derwent Dams, though being at a lower level it has more appeal for the less committed rambler. To the east of the village the country takes on a different aspect as it approaches the junction between the gritstone and limestone. Combs, near Chapel-en-le-Frith, provides the last reservoir before the limestone plateau where the only way of saving water was the building of dewponds, still a common sight in the fields of the central Peak. The villages of Chapel-en-le-Frith and Chinley give access to fine views of the imposing Kinder Scout Plateau to the north.

1. WHALEY BRIDGE

A short circular walk around Whaley Bridge, taking in mixed and coniferous woodland, a reservoir and a canal.

Distance: 3 miles (4.5km).

Allow: 2 hours.

Map: Peak District Touring Map, Dark Peak (sections).

How to get there

By car: Whaley Bridge is on the A5004 half a mile off the A6 Manchester to Derby road. There is a public car park next to the railway station, outside the Jodrell Arms public house.

By bus: service 198/199 from Stockport or Buxton every 30 minutes. Service 252 from Manchester, Nottingham, Matlock or Buxton every 2 hours.

By train: an hourly service operates from Manchester to Buxton, or Buxton to Manchester.

Refreshments: there are a number of public houses in Whaley Bridge, including the Jodrell Arms, Railway Hotel, Goyt and White Hart, all of which are convenient. There is a café near the White Hart.

Start at the car park outside the Jodrell Arms and walk right along Whaley Lane. Just past the railway bridge turn left along Reservoir Road and follow the road alongside the reservoir on your left. Toddbrook Reservoir is a popular calling place for a number of local birds, and coot , mallard, moorhen and the occasional dipper may all be spotted here. After passing a stone gateway turn right though the deciduous woodland. The woods are home to a variety of native birds such as the blue tit, chaffinch, dunnock and green woodpecker, while summer visitors include the redstart and spotted flycatcher.

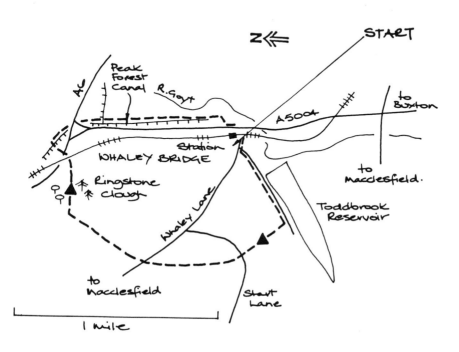

Cross a stile and follow the wall on your right upfield to a fence. At the fence turn to the right through a gate and go between the houses to emerge on Start Lane. Turn left along the lane, then almost immediately right onto a path with a wall on your right hand side. Keeping the wall on your right follow the path over a stile/gate and on to a second one. Once over the second stile turn to the right and cross a further stile. With the wall on your left follow the path to a road, then straight across, again with the wall to your left. After passing a further wall cross a stile to emerge halfway along a large field. Aim for the far left hand corner of the field, rejoining the left hand wall along the way. Go through the gate, and following a short rise turn right off the track at the stile down a long field to emerge in a mixed woodland at another stile.

While deep plantations of conifers inhibit birds, their edges or small plantations attract several species. Amongst the smaller species is the coal tit, which may be distinguished by the white patch on its nape.

The crossbill may also be spotted in conifers, and is obvious by its beak adaptation which allows it to pick seeds out of cones. A high pitched call of "zi zi zi " indicates the presence of another very small bird, the goldcrest.

Crossbill

Continue down the path which widens and improves and cross the works yard ahead. Cross the main road ahead, then cross the footbridge to join the towpath of the Peak Forest Canal. At the canal junction cross another footbridge and follow the towpath onwards into Whaley Bridge and back to your start point.

2. BUXWORTH

A short circular walk connecting the villages of Whaley Bridge and Buxworth, with a return along the Peak Forest Canal.

Distance: 2.5 miles (4 km)

Allow: 1 hour

Map: Peak District Touring Map, Dark Peak

How to get there

Follow directions for route 1, Whaley Bridge

Refreshments: in addition to the pubs mentioned in route 1 there is another, The Navigation, by the canal at Buxworth.

Starting from the car park at the Jodrell Arms, cross the A5004 and walk down Bridge Street past The Goyt public house. Cross the River Goyt and turn right up the incline, a remnant of the former Cromford & High Peak Railway, to join the minor road near a pub, The Shepherd's Arms Inn. Turn left near the pub and continue uphill along Bings Road to an alleyway opposite the church. On reaching the top, the road splits with the left hand fork going to Throstledale and the right hand fork leading upwards to the cricket pitch. Follow the right hand fork, passing the interesting geological phenomenon, The Roosdyche, to your left amongst the trees.

Continue over a cattle grid, passing the cricket pitch to your left, to a lane on your left between Horwich House and Sunart. Follow this lane with a thin line of trees on your right hand side, passing the entrance to Mosley Hall Farm on your left. As the line of trees turns to the east continue north-east keeping the wall on your left to a junction of two paths. The left hand path heads steeply down to join Western Lane and the village of Buxworth. At Western Lane turn left and follow the road downwards to the new bridge and canal basin, where you arrive at The Navigation public house.

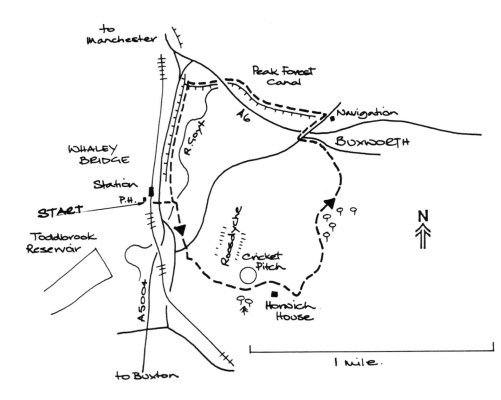

Turn left at the Navigation, or west if you have stopped for a drink, and follow the towpath past a single house, Canal House, and a line of cottages. The towpath continues long this arm of the canal to a junction with the Whaley Bridge arm. Cross the footbridge to emerge on the left hand bank of the canal and continue back to Whaley Bridge, via the wharf and boatyard. At this point it is possible to investigate some of the colourful barges that now use this canal for pleasure cruises. From the wharf it is a short walk, past another Navigation pub, to the main road and the Jodrell Arms.

While this walk does not display the variety of habitats and wildlife exhibited in route 1 there is still much of interest. It is well worth reading further on the history of the Peak Forest Canal and the Cromford and High Peak Railway. The Roosdyche is also extremely interesting, and further reading is again suggested.

Canal Barge at Whaley Bridge

With luck it is possible to spot both mountain hare and stoat on the section between Mosley Hall Farm and Buxworth, while the trees along the route play host to a variety of birds including the meadow pipit.

3. ECCLES PIKE

A medium distance walk with a 700ft (210m) climb through open countryside to Eccles Pike, a 6 acre National Trust property with spectacular views to all sides.

Distance: 5.5 miles (9km)

Allow: 3 hours

Map: Peak District Touring Map, Dark Peak

How to get there

Follow directions for route 1

Refreshments: numerous pubs in Whaley Bridge.

From the Jodrell Arms car park, cross the main road (A5004) and proceed down Bridge Street, crossing the River Goyt by way of the old iron footbridge. From here the railway incline heads off to the right, and a path leads left. Take the left hand path, keeping the river to your left, and continue along the obvious path past the north end of Bings Wood. At the end of this ancient deciduous woodland pass between the edge of the trees (right) and the water (left) to cross first a large field, then a smaller one by way of stiles. The path here joins the Buxworth to Horwich End road, where you turn left, passing a telephone box.

After the last house on the right take the stile into a field, aiming for the next field at a gap in the wall. The path continues via a stile in one of the region's few wire fences. In addition to the aesthetic qualities of a true dry-stone wall, it offers many environmental and economic advantages over wire fencing. The drystone walls of the Peak provide a useful habitat for a number of ground nesting bird species, and provide access for smaller animals. Experiments at the Cheshire Agricultural College, near Nantwich, have shown that the ability to use walls as shelter has increased yields in both sheep and cattle, so making up for the initial outlay of providing a wall, compared to the minimal protection, but low

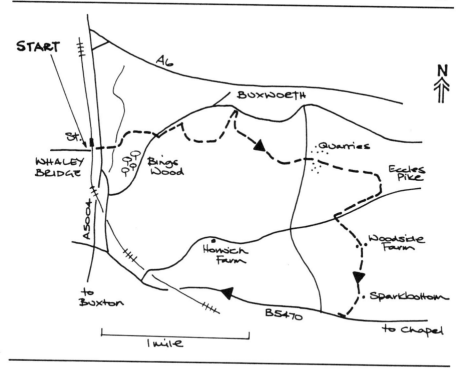

From the fence follow the path to join the wall on your left, crossing two further stiles and a gate to re-emerge at a road. Follow the road uphill with a sharp right turn, and continue as it rapidly becomes a green lane, ending at a gate. Ignoring the two paths ahead turn left through a gap in the wall, then right alongside a wall for a few yards. Leaving the wall behind follow the path across the field, aiming for the south-east corner at the tree line. Along this path, which disintegrates into obscurity, isolated hawthorns stand out and provide fruit for a variety of birds.

At the corner of the field a stile gives access to a sharp climb with a wall on the right. After the next stile cross the field diagonally to reach the road. From here the path splits, with the left hand branch heading to Eccles Fold, and the right hand branch leading down a green lane. Take the right hand branch, passing some old quarries, and after the third boundary wall on your right the path leads steeply up to Eccles Pike. The woodland here was donated to the National Trust in 1937 to commemorate the coronation of King George VI, and is one of the

region's finest viewpoints, with a commanding outlook over the lower
Goyt Valley, Combs Reservoir, and Chinley Churn to the north.

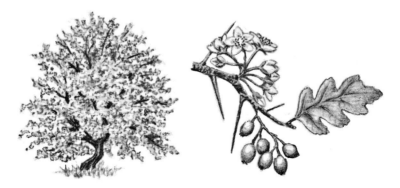

Hawthorn, blossom and berries

While sycamore, ash and hawthorn have
provided the trees up to this point
here the greenery is provided by
conifers. The blue tit, chaffinch and
wren of the deciduous trees give
way to coal tits and crossbill, and it
is well worth pausing here to admire
the view and listen to the sounds of
some of Britain's less common bird life.

From the far side of Eccles Pike turn left
along the road to a stile (left) 200 yards
before Hill Top Farm. From here move
diagonally down hill to the south-east, crossing
a further stile, to join a wall on your left leading
to Woodside Farm. Pass between the old buildings and the new, where a track heads left to
Bradshaw Hall. Ignore this track, but head straight   *Blue Tit*
on, keeping to the left of the stream, to arrive at
Sparkbottom. Here a stile in the wall leads out to the main road between
Whaley Bridge and Chapel-en-le-Frith at the Rose and Crown public
house. From this point there is a half hourly bus service (198/199) back
to the Railway Station at Whaley Bridge, and your starting point.

4. WINDGATHER ROCKS

An easy walk to the last of the gritstone edges before the Cheshire Plain, providing fine views of the vale of Kettleshulme.

Distance: 6 miles (9.5Km.)

Allow: 3 hours 30 minutes

Maps: Peak District Touring Maps, Dark Peak and White Peak

How to get there

Follow directions for route 1.

Refreshments: there are numerous pubs in Whaley Bridge.

From the car park outside the Jodrell Arms take the road leading right, under the railway bridge, then first left up Reservoir Road. Pass the entrance to the park on your left and continue uphill to the dam at Toddbrook Reservoir, where a left turn will lead onto the dam itself.

The three most common birds to be seen all year round at Toddbrook are the mallard, moorhen and coot. While the mallard is readily recognisable by its green head, white neck ring and purple-brown breast in the male, and blue and white wing bar on the female, the coot and moorhen are quite similar in appearance. The easy way to distinguish between the two is by the colour of the bill, red for the moorhen and white for the coot.

Pass across the dam to a stile on the right, and an obvious path leading to a farm. Continue past the farm to a series of recently built houses, where a left turn will bring you to the main road to Macclesfield. Cross the road and take the signposted track ahead, aiming for the top right corner of the field. Cross the drive ahead, followed by a stream, then continue through a narrow belt of trees behind the gardens to emerge on the roadside by Taxal church.

From the church follow the road past Glebe Farm and the rectory to a path on your left. Follow this path past an area of woodland to enter an old deciduous wood by the stile. The dominant tree in this area is the beech, though fine specimens of ash, elm, birch and sycamore abound. Continue through the trees, accompanied by the distinctive "yaffle" call of the green woodpecker, to the River Goyt. Pass alongside the river to a stile on your right hand side, passing a footbridge and stile on your left. From the stile turn right, uphill, via a series of stone steps, to a further stile.

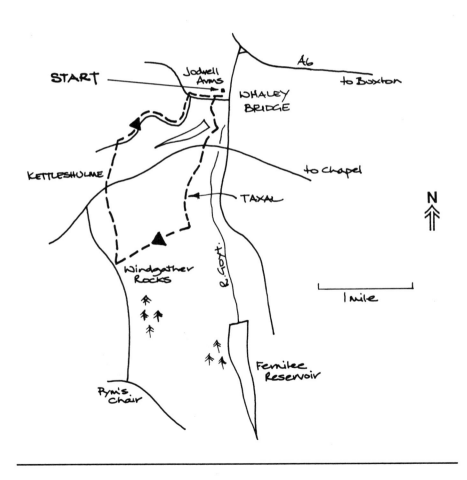

At this point the path curves left in the direction of a small farm, which is soon passed on your left by way of the two gates. Leave the path as it joins a farm road, then turn right through a further gate and continue uphill. After passing a farm to your right take a right hand fork where the road splits, and continue to a junction. The path opposite leads uphill to the top of the ridge.

Beech Tree with (inset) leaf and fruit

Walk alongside the obvious plantation to a stile, then continue as the path undulates first down, then up, through small deciduous groves. At a further stile, on your left, leave the trees and follow the path alongside a drystone wall to the final stile before Windgather Rocks. The rocks here are an important training area for the rock climbers of the region, and were the early learning ground of some of Britain's finest climbers. Summer evenings are best if you wish to watch people in action on the rocks, though beware of tripping over ropes or disturbing equipment. Though the climbers may make the sport appear simple it should not be tried without proper equipment and supervision from an experienced leader. From the top of Windgather the views are particularly impressive, with the Cheshire Plain stretching away below. Down to the right is the village of Kettleshulme, and your route back to Whaley Bridge.

Leaving the edge to your left cross into a long field with a wall on your left, and so down to a gate. Here pass through the farmyard by turning left, then right, and on through a further field to a stile. Cross the field diagonally to your left to join a lane via the stile. Continue down the lane to a left turn, just after an "S" bend, where a long thin field curves to your left. The path continues downhill, crossing a stile and a stream along the way. Passing the farm to your left follow the path round to your right and onto the driveway of Bent Hall Farm. Pass the farm and continue on down to the main road, curving left as you go. At the main road cross straight over onto the road mentioned in route 1, Start Lane. This may be followed to its junction with Whaley Lane, where a right turn leads directly back to the car park at Whaley Bridge.

5. FERNILEE

A medium difficulty walk connecting the reservoirs of Fernilee and Combs, with easy sections along the waterside and hard climbs onto the farmland between Whaley Bridge and Buxton.

Distance: 9 miles (14.5km)

Allow: 4 hours

Maps: Peak District Touring Map, White Peak

How to get there

By car: from Whaley Bridge take the B5470 towards Chapel-en-le-Frith to the Rose and Crown Pub at Tunstead Milton.

Bus: services 198/199 as mentioned in route 1

Refreshments: The Rose and Crown at Tunstead Milton and the Shady Oak on Long Hill (A5004).

Start from the car park at the Rose and Crown pub and walk east towards Chapel-en-le-Frith. After a few yards a signposted stile on the right leads left to a small stream, which is followed to the embankment of Combs Reservoir. A series of steps leads to a road running below the embankment, then a bridge over the railway line. The road now continues past Meveril Farm to Tunstead Farm. From the rear of Tunstead Farm turn right along a track which leads to open fields.

The wall ahead is crossed by means of a ladder stile and a fork is reached, where the left hand branch is taken to an old reservoir. Keep the wall to your left and continue to the end of the reservoir till a left turn after a stile is taken to Elnor Lane. On reaching the road turn left once more, passing the houses to another fork. The right hand branch is now followed down to the Shady Oak at Fernilee by way of a right turn just prior to the church.

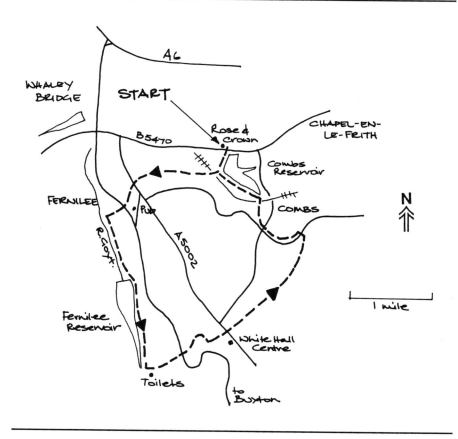

Cross the A5004 to a track which leads down through the buildings of Folds Lane Farm then heads diagonally left through open fields to a footbridge. This crosses a minor stream and leads to another, concrete, bridge. Turn left at the beginning of the bridge and follow the side of the river. At the water treatment works by the foot of Fernilee Reservoir take the old works road, which climbs steeply to the top of the embankment. The path ahead is followed along the route of the Cromford and High Peak Railway, which is used frequently throughout walks in this area.

The railway track is left at Bunsal Cob, the obvious hill at the junction of Fernilee and Errwood Reservoirs. By the side of the toilets a stile on your left leads downhill to a stream and footbridge, then steeply uphill in the direction of the main road. At the cross roads of paths go directly ahead, along an obvious track, then follow it round to the right and its junction with Long Hill.

Cross the road and follow the path ahead to the junction of a drive connecting North Lodge and the White Hall Centre for Open Country Pursuits, a county council run centre used for teaching outdoor activities. A left turn here leads behind the centre to an offset crossroads, where you go straight across onto an old roman road. After a few yards take a left turn up a track which drops steeply towards Broadlee farm. Pass the farm to your right and continue onwards to a footbridge where two streams meet. The path now climbs again to join a minor road passing Allstone Lee (right) before reaching Rye Flat Farm.

Pass through the farm to join a road, then turn left to Combs village. Walk though the village, keeping to the same road, then take the first path on your right, just past the end of the wooded railway embankment. Cross the railway and then branch left where the path forks, to emerge on the banks of Combs Reservoir. From here continue alongside the reservoir to reach the embankment at the road, where a right turn leads you back to the main B5470 and your starting point.

The sections of this walk between the Cromford and High Peak Railway and Rye Flat Farm are among the most natural encountered in this section of the western Peak. Care should be taken here, where the ground can be particularly wet and boggy, especially in winter. It is not uncommon to see mountain hares along this section, and a keen eye may also take in the equally nervous stoat.

The sections of stream feeding into either the reservoirs of the Goyt Valley, or Combs, also make good ground for studying some of the macro-invertebrate life of the peak. Stone-fly and may-fly provide an important part in the local food chain, providing a source of food for fish such as trout and grayling. The river lamprey is also relatively common, feeding on organic debris brought down by the waters flowing off the moorlands.

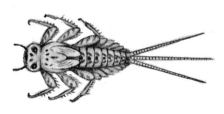

Mayfly

6. CRACKEN EDGE

A short walk with a stiff climb up to Cracken Edge, then a more gentle descent winding back into Chinley

Distance: 5 Miles (8km)

Allow: 2 hours 30 minutes

Maps: Peak District Touring Map, Dark Peak

How to get there

By car: Chinley lies on the B6062 and may be reached via the A6 Manchester – Derby road from the Chapel-en-le-Frith bypass by turning at Bridgemont (Whaley Bridge end). Alternatively the A624 Glossop – Chapel road may be taken.

By bus: service 181 from Buxton or Whaley Bridge.

By train: regular Services operate between Manchester Piccadilly and Chinley on the Hope Valley/Sheffield line.

Refreshments: public houses at Chinley and the Crown and Mitre at New Smithy (just off the route).

From Chinley walk up Whitehough Road to the junction with Stubbins Lane, where a left turn leads you past Chinley Railway Station. Leave the village behind as the road begins to climb, and ignore the first path which leaves to your right just after a right hand bend. Once past Dryclough Farm a signpost indicates a stile to your right and the path onwards. The path continues to climb alongside a wall (right) to a fence topped wall and stile. Beyond the stile the path traverses rough ground below the old quarries of Cracken Edge.

The quarries here supplied a large quantity of roofing slate in former times, and both the workings and old mine entrances are still obvious. Although many large rocks litter the base of the quarry, the best quality slates were gained by means of deep adits driven into the base of the outcrop. The workings have long been closed, but the remains of an old winding engine still exist at the far end of the quarry, and many of the older buildings in the area exhibit the hard-won slate as roofing.

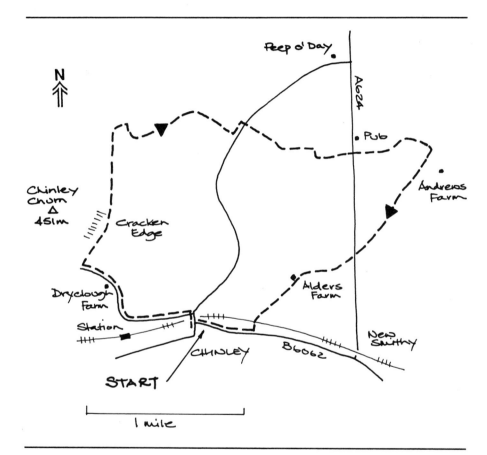

Beyond the winding engine the track improves considerably as it progresses downhill towards Hills Farm. At the cross roads in the paths, with the main track ahead going to Whiterakes House, turn right. The path turns right towards a small deciduous coppice, then left towards the far corner of the field. Continue diagonally left to a stile just before the corner of the field, then follow the wall on your right down through two more fields to join the road from Chinley to Peep O' Day (or Hills House, depending on which map you have).

Turn left along the road for a few yards, to a path on your right which crosses two minor streams forming Otter Brook. Once into the next field keep the wall to your left while following it round to Monk's Meadows. Cross the stile ahead and then, still with the wall to your left, progress to the main road (A624). Cross the road and follow the right hand wall to the far corner of the field, and a stile. The path here cuts diagonally left across the field and then, beyond the stile, curves right to another wall and a junction in paths. Take the right hand track which drops down to the A624 once more, passing tracks to Andrews Farm and Bradshaw Fields (left) and a disused quarry (left). Cross the road and progress down to Alders Farm, which is passed on your right. The path ahead crosses Otter Brook once more, then becomes a wide track down to the B6062 just east of Chinley. A right turn here leads directly back to the village and your starting point.

7. FURNESS VALE

A short walk that combines stiff climbing up to the moors above Chinley with a long section of the Peak Forest Canal.

Distance: 6 miles (9.5km)

Allow: 2 hours 30 minutes

Maps: Peak District Touring Map, Dark Peak

How to get there

Follow directions for walk 6 (Cracken Edge).

Refreshments: there are pubs in Chinley, Furness Vale and Buxworth, all of which lie within easy reach of this route.

The route starts from the War Memorial on Stubbins Lane at Chinley, where parking is available. Walk west along the road, out of the village, and past the railway station (left). Take the fourth path to leave the road on the right, passing the Cracken Edge route along the way, and climb steeply up the obvious track. The first two fields are full of trial holes dug deep into the underlying millstone grit. Trial holes are a common sight in the northern Peak due to the proximity of the underlying coal measures, particularly along the flanks of the Derbyshire Dome.

Pass alongside these holes through the first two, narrow fields, and into a third which is wider and contains fewer trials. Continue to rise, aiming for the centre of the wall ahead, and so into another field divided by telegraph poles.

At this point it is not uncommon to spot mountain hares. These animals are extremely shy, and except in winter are difficult to distinguish from their relative, the common or brown hare. The easiest method of quick identification is to note the length and size of the ears. A large mountain hare can be as big as a small specimen of the common hare, but its ears will always be smaller and shorter. If the fur appears to be more

Mountain Hare

blue-grey than brown, you can be almost certain of your sighting, and in winter the white fur is a method of certain identification.

It should be remembered, though, that its generic name *lepus timidus* is well chosen, and your sighting is likely to be short lived due to its natural wariness of humans.

Beyond the telegraph poles a junction in the path is reached, with the right hand path heading down to join route 6. At the junction turn left, continuing through the rough moorland as you descend steeply in the direction of New Mills. The fields around you are full of a variety of native plant species, and bilberry, crowberry and soft rush are evident everywhere. The ground is

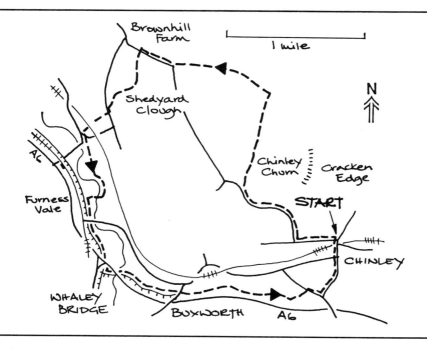

also a lot damper at this point, with streams on the right feeding the River Sett, and those on the left joining the lower reaches of the River Goyt.

The next junction brings you out at the continuation of the road out of Chinley, now called Over Hill Road, though it has deteriorated somewhat. Ignoring this, continue ahead along Laneside Road, using Brownhill Farm as a guide. After 400 yards take the track heading left, which leads down to Shedyard Farm. The next 600 yards lie alongside a minor tributary of the Goyt called Shedyard Clough, lined by trees on your left, to a further junction. Turn left here, followed by a right turn just past the trees, and walk under the electricity pylons aiming for the wall ahead, slightly left of the railway embankment. Once under the railway line you cross under the pylons again and join a road close to a junction. The right hand fork leads down to a sharp right turn, where a path leaves to join the River Goyt. If a refreshment break is required, following the road round this bend leads quickly into Furness Vale. It should be noted that the railway station here is not on a direct line to Chinley, so is unsuitable for a short cut unless you are prepared to go back to New Mills and change trains.

From the bend in the road, follow the path down by the side of the river for a few yards. The path cuts off a left hand meander in the river, before rejoining it at a right hand bend opposite the sewage works. Beyond this bend you reach a junction at Peathill, where aright turn leads over a footbridge to the Peak Forest Canal. This is then followed, keeping the water to your right, down to a canal junction where the Whaley Bridge arm continues ahead.

The left hand branch of the canal provides your route onwards, as mentioned in route 2 (Buxworth), as far as the Navigation public house at Buxworth. Continue from the pub along the bed of the old tramway, with Black Brook to your left and the bypass to your right. After a mile you reach the back of the White Hall works, where you exit via the driveway to join a minor road. Cross this road along the tramway, to reach Whitehough Road by the side of a small electricity substation. From here a left turn leads back through the village to your start point at the war memorial.

8. SOUTH HEAD

A long, undulating walk culminating at South Head, with fine views over Chinley and Chapel-en-le-Frith.

Distance: 7.5 miles (12km)

Allow: 2 hours 30 minutes

Maps: Peak District Touring Map, Dark Peak

How to get there

By car: Chapel-en-le-Frith lies just off the main A6 Manchester – Derby road, and may be reached by turning off the bypass at either the A624 or A625 junctions.

By train: a regular, hourly service is operated throughout the year between Manchester Piccadilly and Chapel-en-le-Frith, on the Buxton line.

By bus: regular services operate between Chapel and either Manchester, Stockport or Buxton. Services 198/199 operate every half hour, and service 252 operates every 2 hours.

Refreshments: Chapel is well served by public houses, including the Shoulder of Mutton, The Old Pack Horse and the New Inn. There is also a café on the market place.

The walk starts from the market place at the centre of Chapel-en-le-Frith, though parking may be difficult. If the market place is full, or a market is open (Thursdays) alternative parking is available at the car park on Thornbrook Road, 200 yards east.

From the market place turn left along the main B5470 in the direction of Buxton. Pass the Shoulder of Mutton public house on your left and cross the road at the pedestrian crossing. Continue along to Ashbourne Lane on your right hand side, just prior to Longsons and the A6 turn off.Follow Ashbourne Lane till just after the end of the houses, and a

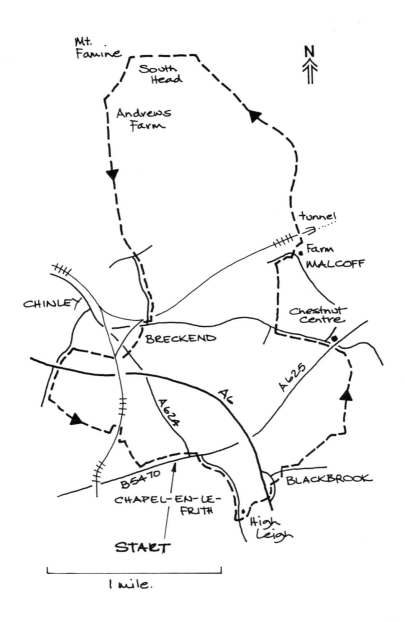

footpath on your left which takes you behind High Leigh. The path is narrow and walled on each side, but not difficult to locate.

Continue along the obvious track, and under the electricity power lines close to a pylon. A left turn near a gate will lead you down, via a stile, to the road. This must be crossed with extreme caution, to reach the path on the opposite side. From here a series of steps and a stile give access to a footbridge over the stream. The path now leads directly into the small hamlet of Blackbrook, and a minor road leading towards Sparrowpit.

Turn right along the Sparrowpit road, climbing through trees as you go, to another series of steps on either side. Turn left up the steps and into the field ahead. The path bends slightly to the right before joining a larger track coming in from the left. Follow this track right, and continue through Bagshaw Hall Farm to the beginning of Bagshaw hamlet. Your next landmark is a phone box on the left, where a path leaves the road and climbs up through the fields to emerge by the side of Maglow Farm. Keep to the right of the farm buildings and progress though two stiles and a gate to a road.

Turn left here, then immediately left again as you reach the A625. Ahead of you is the Chestnut Centre, an animal and bird sanctuary which is open to the public, and well worth a visit. Its main activity is the preservation of owls and otters. Cross the road and continue through Slackhall, another small hamlet.

Left: Tawny Owl; right: Kestrel

Where a road exits left at Bowden Head turn directly right, opposite the road turn off, and follow the wall on your left hand side. At the corner of the field access is possible to Bowdenhead Wood. This is an ideal opportunity to differentiate between the two types of woodland common to the Peak. Bowdenhead Wood is a typical, small, deciduous woodland, while just to your right is the coniferous plantation of Birchenlow. The path now runs left through the trees before a right turn exits the woods. From this point the path rises steadily, crossing a stream via a footbridge, to join the road and a right turn into Malcoff.

Just prior to Malcoff Farm a path leads off to the left, and a series of stone steps gives access to the corner of a field. The path now bends sharply to your left and heads for the railway line close to the famous Cowburn Tunnel. This is the longest railway tunnel in the Peak, being over one and a quarter miles long, and is an astonishing sight when travelling from Manchester to Sheffield on the Hope Valley line. The landscape prior to the tunnel is a series of rolling hills and valleys, but once through the other end, you emerge into the true Dark Peak, close to Edale and the base of the imposing Kinder Scout Plateau.

Cross the railway by way of the bridge, and ascend the steep, and wet, bank ahead. Either of the two paths ahead may be followed, but the left hand one follows the wall and is commonly drier. The farm ahead is Shireoaks, a true misnomer as the trees are in fact sycamores. Although this is a common tree it is not, in fact, native to this country. It is most easily identifiable by the combination of its five-pointed, deep green, leaves and its fruit. These fruit are the well-known "helicopters" much loved by children.

Keep the buildings of Shireoaks to your left and climb the bank ahead of you to join part of the system of ancient packhorse routes. These packhorse routes were the "roadways" of ancient times, prior to the invention of the motor car, and make fine walking. This particular one runs from near Perryfoot in a north westerly direction to Mount Famine, and beyond. Their importance as major traffic routes is obvious by the size of the gate ahead: the five foot width was almost exactly right for a fully laden packhorse.

As you walk along the track the views to your right are up the flanks of Brown Knoll, at 1849ft (569m) the true start of the northern moorlands.

Sycamore; inset. leaf and 'helicopter' fruit

Here the rough moorland is full of bracken, a rapidly growing, wild plant that is providing particular concern of late. Once in place bracken is extremely difficult to dislodge from its niche as it grows underground from a dark creeping stem.

The packhorse track now leads onwards to reach South Head, a fine vantage point, with views to the south and west. Eccles Pike, Chinley Churn and Ladder Hill are all visible from here. Continue past a path leading off right to the River Sett, and reach another junction, this time with a track left. Take this left turn, and walk down the steep bank past some old quarries to emerge at a four way junction in the paths. The right hand path leads to the A624, emerging close to a pub, but the way on is left and down to Andrews Farm.

Pass to the right of the house, between the buildings, and on through a gate. The path now descends steeply past Bullhill and Dewsnaps to finally reach a road junction. A right turn here leads to New Smithy, and the Crown and Mitre pub, though the route again moves ahead down a minor road. Follow this road down to its junction at Breckend, where you turn right before crossing over the road to take the footpath left. This path continues, crossing the twin railway lines, and arrives at a mill. From here turn left down Charley Lane, under the bypass, to a path on your left. Follow this path, with the wall on your left, across two fields. Pass the buildings of The Course on your left and through three further fields. A sharp left hand turn followed by two sharp rights will see you safely through to the other side of the railway line, and the path back to the centre of Chapel.

Buxton and the Goyt Valley

Buxton is the largest town in the area and is central to the western Peak, though lying outside the park boundaries itself due to the large number of limestone quarries in the vicinity. In summer the town is a tourist trap, with attractions ranging from the Roman Baths, which use natural spa water, to an Opera House and fine Georgian architecture. The town even has its own country park, where a series of walks through mature woodland lead to a folly, Solomon's Temple, with fine views over the town and its surroundings.

Two miles outside Buxton lies the Goyt Valley, perhaps the most popular spot in the area for day trippers and picnics. It had become so popular that by the early seventies the Peak Park Joint Planning Board were forced to introduce a system of traffic regulation to save the valley from overcrowding. The section between the end of Errwood Reservoir and Derbyshire Bridge is now only accessible from Long Hill by car. The river valley was dammed in the thirties to create the twin reservoirs of Fernilee and Errwood, and with the provision of large car parks and picnic sites it makes an ideal site for family walking, or a starting point for access to some of the more strenuous moorland rambles. The wide scale planting of coniferous and mixed woodland helps to protect the valley from the wind, while combining with the open water to attract a wide diversity of bird species.

Beyond the plantations to the west lies the classic ridge walk from Pym's Chair to Shining Tor. This is well worth walking if only for the impressive views it offers. On a fine day it is easy to pick out the radio telescopes of Jodrell Bank, while across the Cheshire Plain you can see the Berwyn Mountains in the distance. Continuing south from Shining Tor past the Cat & Fiddle Inn you meet the true moors and Axe Edge. This is the preserve of the Red Grouse, where heather and ling replace the grass and trees of the valley, and your companions are more likely to be the Derbyshire Gritstone Sheep than human beings. Axe Edge is also an important watershed with streams flowing off its flanks to loin either the Mersey or the Trent. Four important rivers, The Manifold, Dove, Dane and Goyt all rise on Axe Edge, and all provide walks for this book.

9. FERNILEE RESERVOIR

A short, flat walk around Fernilee Reservoir in the Goyt Valley.

Distance: 3.25 miles (5km)

Allow: 1 hour 30 minutes

Maps: Peak District Touring Map, White Peak

How to get there

By car: the Goyt Valley is only accessible from Long Hill, the A5002 Buxton to Whaley Bridge Road, north west of Buxton.

By train: the nearest railway station is at Buxton, 4 miles away. Trains run hourly to and from Manchester Piccadilly.

By bus: Buxton is the nearest main centre, with a large number of services from the north west.

Refreshments: the Goyt Valley has no pubs or cafés, the nearest pub being the Shady Oak on Long Hill. In summer a number of ice cream vans serve the valley.

The starting point for this, and many of the Goyt Valley walks, is The Street Car Park between Errwood and Fernilee Reservoirs. The car park has a useful information board, containing information on both the Goyt Valley and the Roman road which leads from the car park up to the vantage point at Pym's Chair.

From the car park take the short section of road down to the embankment dividing the two dams. Just before turning on to the dam turn left by a small plantation, and head through a gap in the wall into the plantation. The majority of the trees here are coniferous, though odd examples of beech may be located. As you progress through the plantation it is worth studying the cones from the various pine trees. Each cone is slightly different in shape, and provides a useful means of identifying different species where an overall view of a tree is restricted.

The main varieties of conifer found in the peak are the larch, pine and spruce. The larch has an oval cone with rounded seeds. The pine cone is more tapering towards the lower end, and has very elongated wings to the seeds. The spruce cone is more of a rounded rectangle in shape and has seeds of a similar nature, rounded towards the end of each wing.

Cones and seeds – Larch (top left), Spruce (centre) and Scots Pine (bottom)

The path leads alongside the banks of the reservoir and crosses a number of feeder streams, the first being Jep Clough. Beyond Jep Clough the path divides, and the left hand fork provides the route onwards. A further, un-named stream is passed, with beech trees to the left, before a

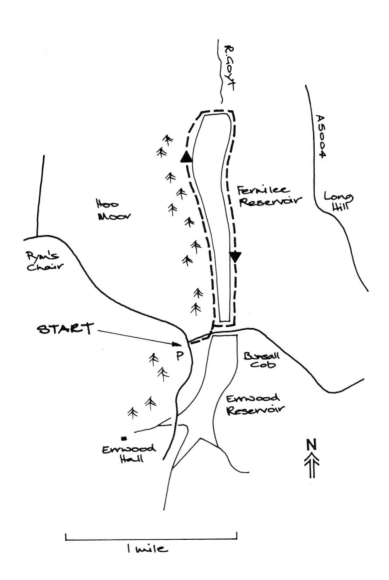

footbridge is reached. This crosses Deep Clough, approximately half way along the reservoir. From the footbridge the path bends to the right, and then to the left to keep parallel to the reservoir bank. Keep the wall to your left for a short while, and when the path deviates from it you are approaching the end of the reservoir. Two further, minor, streams are crossed to allow you to exit from the plantation. The path now turns quite sharply to the right, allowing you to reach the embankment at the Whaley Bridge end of Fernilee.

Progress across the embankment, then turn right onto the bed of the disused railway line. The bank on your left now rises steeply to the A5002. Continue along the disused railway, past a track leading up to the road (the way to the Shady Oak) constantly keeping the reservoir to your right. A short section of trees, mainly beech, leads to an incline at the end of the embankment. From here a right turn leads back onto the road crossing between Errwood and Fernilee. Right here soon brings you back to the Street car park, and your starting point.

This walk is only short, and level throughout ninety per cent of its length, but it provides a superb contrast between the wide open waters of Fernilee and the dark plantations lining the eastern bank of Hoo Moor. Both the plantations and the waterside provide habitats for a variety of bird species as mentioned previously in this book. Being a shorter distance walk it allows time to study these different species in the safety of a secluded valley. While Fernilee Reservoir and the northern end of the Goyt Valley are by no means unpopular, they do not attract the same number of visitors as the more popular Errwood Reservoir.

10. PYM'S CHAIR

A superb walk showing the contrasts between the dark coniferous plantation along Fernilee Reservoir and the open moors alongside the ridge from Windgather to Pym's Chair.

Distance: 5.25 miles (8.5km)

Allow: 2 hours 30 minutes

Maps: Peak District Touring Map, White Peak

How to get there

Follow the directions for route 9 (Fernilee Reservoir)

Refreshments: there are no pubs or cafés nearby, though in summer the valley is well served by ice cream vans.

The starting point, and early part of the route, is that used in the previous route, around the western flank of Fernilee Reservoir. From The Street Car Park walk down to the embankment, where a left turn by a small plantation leads through a hole in the wall to the side of the reservoir. Follow the previous route through the trees, again keeping left at the fork by a gate, and onwards to the bridge over Deep Clough.

Beyond the footbridge follow the path to where it leaves the plantation. Where the previous route turned right for the embankment you turn left, with a wall on your right hand side. At the end of the wall the path curves right, between two walls, then left (wall on your left), to a straight short straight section. The path then executes two zigzags, crossing Mill Clough and passing two cottages to your right, before reaching a T-junction.

Turn right, uphill, to pass Overton Hall farm on your right. Cross the path running left to right and continue up through open country to a stile on your left, which enters Goyt Forest. This plantation is almost exclusively spruce, and the age of the trees can be gauged by counting

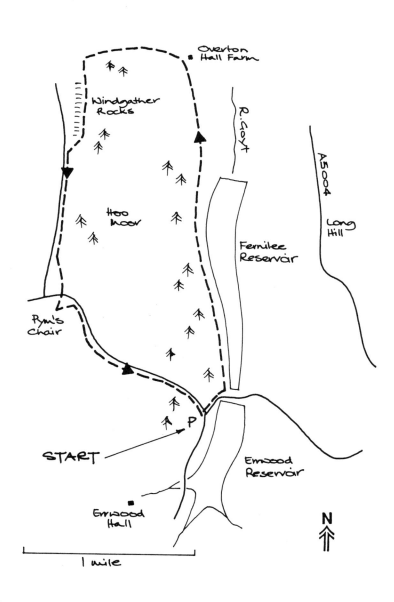

the successive whorls of branches. A spruce tree grows one whorl annually.

Follow the wall on your left, and cross a stile. The wall is now on your right, and leads via another stile to the top of Windgather rocks. The next mile is along the county boundary between Derbyshire and Cheshire, with impressive views west over the Cheshire Plain. As mentioned in the section on walks around Whaley Bridge, these rocks are an important training ground for rock climbers.

Follow the line of Windgather rocks, a most appropriate name due to its exposure, then cross a stile onto a path running alongside the road. With the road to your right, and Goyt Forest to your left, continue to a fork in the paths. Take the left fork here, to join the Roman road leading downhill (left) to the Street car park. A right turn up the road leads quickly to another major viewpoint, Pym's Chair. The views are again over the Cheshire Plain, and into the Vale of Kettleshulme, but you now have the advantage of a further 150ft in height. To the left is the ridge walk over to Shining Tor.

Turn back to where you joined the Roman road, which is then followed downhill. The first half of this road passes through typical rough, open, moorland.

Amongst the plants evident here are crowberry, bilberry and cross leaved heather. The bilberry is a short, deciduous shrub with green twigs and leaves, oval in shape.

Its flowers, visible between April and June, are a pink colour and flask shaped, but it is the fruit which attract most attention. These are round and purple-black in colour, and are edible. They also make exceedingly good wine.

Bilberry

Continue downhill with steep banks to either side, passing the path to Errwood Hall on your right. Shortly after this path the slopes are once more lined with spruce,the left hand side stretching over Hoo Moor and the right leading through to the edge of Errwood Hall. Continue down the road, which bends right as the trees to your left give way to a large open field, and you are back at the car park and your starting point.

Crowberry with, top left, Peacock butterfly and. right, a Red Admiral

11. ERRWOOD HALL

A walk that takes you along the tree lined banks of the upper reaches of the River Goyt, then ascends towards Shining Tor before dropping down to the ruins of Errwood Hall.

Distance: 3.5 miles (5.5km)

Allow: 1 hour 30 minutes

Maps: Peak District Touring Map, White Peak

How to get there:

Follow the directions for route 9 as far as the Street car park, then turn left along the road by the side of Errwood Reservoir to Errwood car park.

Refreshments: as for route 10, there are no refreshments within easy reach of the valley. A short detour half way along the route will allow you to visit the Cat & Fiddle Inn on the Buxton – Macclesfield road.

The starting point is Errwood Car Park at the southern end of the reservoir. This road has a one way system in operation restricting traffic from heading in the direction of the Street. On the road sections of this walk care should be taken as traffic is still allowed towards Derbyshire Bridge, and will therefore be coming from behind you.

From the car park head south along the banks of Errwood Reservoir, using the restricted road. This is where the river Goyt enters the reservoir through a steep valley, lined with trees on your right hand side. The banks high to your right are almost exclusively coniferous, but to your right there is a combination of beech and Scots Pine. Compared to the monotonous rows of spruce found in the previous route these trees make a refreshing change. The Scots Pine is particularly pleasing, being Britain's only native species still grown commercially.

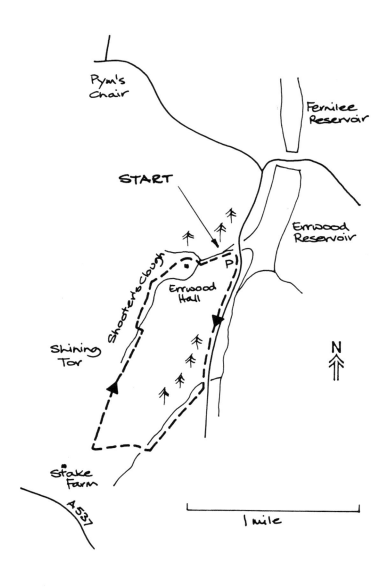

Pym's
Chair

Fernilee
Reservoir

START

Errwood
Reservoir

Shooters Clough

Errwood
Hall

Shining
Tor

N

Stake
Farm

A537

1 mile

Scots Pine

In comparison to the spruce and larch the Scots Pine is easily identifiable. Older trees can be identified by their characteristic orange-brown upper trunk and branches. This actually appears as the bark flakes off. The needles are extremely long in comparison with other commercial species, and grow in pairs. The most recognisable characteristic, however, is their tendency for single sided growth and very few branches at low level.

Continue along the roadway, noting the fast growing expanse of bracken on the opposite bank of the river. Where an obvious track heads off left the roadway moves away from the riverside. 400 yards further on a signposted track heads off to your right, shortly before Goytsclough Quarry. Ascend this track, with deep woods to either side, along the left hand bank of Stake Clough. As you emerge from the trees you arrive at a crossroads in the paths.

The way on here is to your right, across the small stream, and alongside a wall (right). The path now rises more steeply as you leave the trees behind and head into open moorland. A half mile climb brings you to a further crossroads, with Stake Farm ahead and the Macclesfield road to your left. This is the point to leave the route if you wish to take refreshments at the Cat & Fiddle Inn. To continue on the route turn right at the crossroads, with a wall on your left. After a short distance the path up to Shining Tor leaves to your right, but ignore this and continue ahead. The path now starts to descend again through open moorland.

After half a mile you are rejoined by plantations on your left. The path enters the plantation at an offset T junction, and turns sharply to your left. Once through the trees, follow the wall on your right which becomes broken part way along. Shortly after the wall regains its full height a sharp left, followed by a sharp right gets you across Shooter's Clough, and once more into open country. With the stream now to your right descend to the ruins of Errwood Hall. The grounds here are full of a variety of plants, both native and introduced, with rhododendron in particular covering wide areas.

The hall itself lies to your right, and may be seen by either going directly ahead, or turning right, at the path crossroads. The most scenic route is that to your right, which follows Shooter's Clough down to a fork in the paths. Left here brings you to the stream's entry into the reservoir, but the right hand fork arrives at the wall on the far side of Errwood car park, and your starting point.

12. DERBYSHIRE BRIDGE

A walk taking in a full circuit of Errwood Reservoir with a ramble up the upper Goyt to a popular picnic spot.

Distance: 7 miles (11km)

Allow: 2 hours 30 minutes

Maps: White Peak 1:25,000

How to get there

Follow directions for route 11

Refreshments: The Cat & Fiddle pub lies three quarters of a mile to the south west of Derbyshire Bridge.

Starting from Errwood Car Park at the southern end of the reservoir follow the road running south, as for the previous route. This time walk on past the path leading right up Stake Clough, and take a path on the same side just past Goytsclough Quarry. This starts to veer away from the road as it heads into a conifer plantation. After a short distance you meet a path coming in from left to right, and it is here that you turn left with a wall still on your right hand side.

As you leave the plantation, cross a wall into some bracken, followed by a small section of rough ground and a road. Turn right to rejoin the Goyt Valley road, remembering that traffic may be coming from behind you. As you enter Goyt's Clough there is a waterfall on your right where water flows down from Foxhole Hollow to join the river below.

Continue along the road, all the time leaving the river to your left. The road turns to the right, then swings gently left to bring you to Derbyshire Bridge. This is the limit of vehicular access from the Buxton – Macclesfield road. A right turn here leads up to the Cat & Fiddle, and your only chance for a refreshment break. Turn left up the wide track leading past the buildings at Derbyshire Bridge to continue your route.

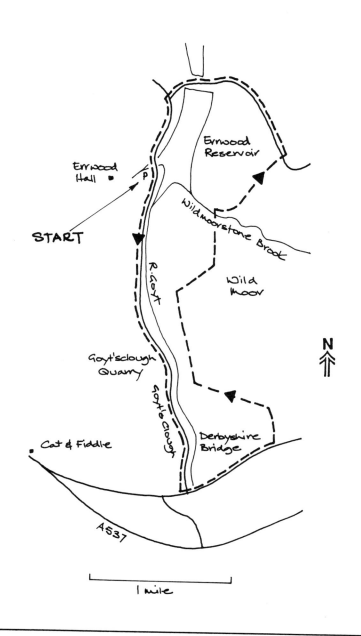

The next half mile is easy walking along a wide path, slowly ascending in the direction of Buxton. Several paths leave to your right, but it is the first path on your left that provides a route back towards Errwood Reservoir. The path leaves the main track at its highest point, and just after the head of Berry Clough. Follow this path north to a T-junction, where you again turn left and begin the steep descent back towards the Goyt. The path now swings right, then left, to cross a minor stream and progress along the right hand bank of Berry Clough. Shortly after crossing another stream you enter a wide area of bracken.

As the path turns to the right it is possible to cross the river and rejoin the road towards Goytsclough Quarry, but for those wishing to go on, follow the path above the river to where it splits. The left hand path continues through thick bracken, but the right hand route is more easily navigable. Continue right from the fork and head across the slope parallel to the river below.

Just as the bracken begins to thicken again you meet a stream, which is crossed, and continue in a straight line to meet a wall running left to right across your path. Cross the wall at the corner of a field, then walk right alongside the wall and away from the river. The bracken has now given way to more open country, and the wall provides a good guideline as you traverse Wild Moor.

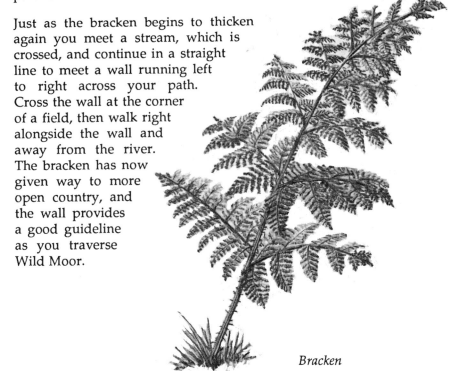

Bracken

Cross the stream ahead, then where you meet a path to your left cross to the other side of the wall and move north east. The next landmark is a 90 degree junction in the wall on your left. Keep on this side of the wall as you turn right then left to cross yet another stream. At the next wall junction cross at the corner and go on to meet Wildmoorstone Brook, one of the major tributaries leading into Errwood Reservoir. The path now crosses the brook and turns right alongside it for a few yards. Follow the minor tributary coming in from your left to emerge at a road. To your right is a triangular pond and another section of the disused Cromford and High Peak Railway. Turn left here to follow the road down into the valley below. This section of road drops steeply along a former railway incline, where the ground was too steep for early trains to manage without outside help.

Pass Bunsal Cob to your left and emerge onto the embankment dividing Errwood and Fernilee Reservoirs. From here a left turn by The Street car park leads along the road back to Errwood car park and your starting point.

13. SHINING TOR

This classic ridge walk from Pym's Chair to Shining Tor gives superb views of the Cheshire Plain, Manchester and the Welsh mountains.

Distance: 5 miles (8km)

Allow: 2 hours

Maps: White Peak 1:25,00

How to get there

Follow directions for route 11

Refreshments: The Cat & Fiddle Inn lies just to the south east of Shining Tor. The Shining Tor Café is below the Cat and Fiddle.

From Errwood take the path directly behind the car park and cross the stile into the woods. Carry on downhill before the path rises and crosses a stream. To your right lie the ruins of Errwood Hall, as mentioned in route 11, but you follow the path straight ahead as it continues to rise. The path turns to the right as you complete a semi-circle around the hall, and eventually emerges from the woodland. Once out of the woods pass between two collapsing walls and turn right onto a wide, grassy path which starts to descend slowly to a stream. Cross the stream and take the left hand path at a junction.

The path in front of you now crosses rough ground between Withinleach Moor and Foxlow Edge. Keep the wall to your left, with small mixed woodlands beyond it, as you move steadily north. If you are walking in summer keep an eye open for one of the most common migrant species of birds in the area, the ring ouzel. This species is a relative of the blackbird and resembles it in many ways. Standing about 24 cm high and having a yellow beak, its main distinguishing feature is the obvious white gorget, a band across the upper chest. If viewed from the rear look for a pale patch on the wing, particularly noticeable in the male.

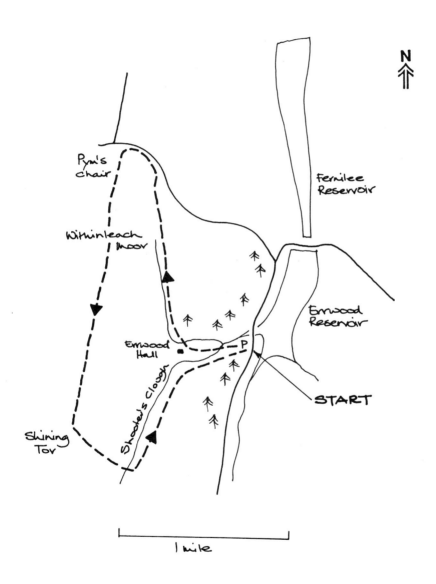

N

Pym's chair

Withinleach moor

Fernilee Reservoir

Errwood Reservoir

Errwood Hall

P

START

Shooter's Clough

Shining Tor

1 mile

Go straight ahead at the crossroads in the paths and you will shortly reach the road coming up from The Street. At this point turn left and continue uphill to an obvious path on the left. This point is Pym's Chair, a superb viewpoint as mentioned previously. Follow this path over the old wall ahead, and onto the ridge. The ridge itself continues for two miles, undulating most of the way. The first summit is called Cats Tor, from which you descend to The Tors. To your left the moors are open, while to your right a series of drystone walls run down in parallel lines towards Lamaload Reservoir and Rainow. From The Tors the path starts to climb again, still running along the line of the Cheshire/Derbyshire county boundary. Ahead lies the obvious summit of Shining Tor, which at a little over 1830ft is the highest point in the area.

From the summit the views are unquestionably the best in the western Peak. To the west lie the Berwyn Mountains, beyond the vast Cheshire Plain. To the north west Manchester is clearly visible, while to the south the landscape is dominated by the radio mast outside the Cat & Fiddle and the imposing watershed of Axe Edge. On a nice summer day this is an ideal place to sit, with large rocks to the west providing a suitable platform. In winter, however, this is a remote and forbidding place, where the wind and rain seem ceaseless. When the wind blows it is certainly no place to hang around, as cloud and mist appear from nowhere and visibility can deteriorate in a matter of minutes.

From the summit of Shining Tor the path heads down to your left alongside a wall (left). As the path begins to rise again you reach a T-junction. Turn left here, again keeping the wall on your left hand side, as you descend steadily into Shooter's Clough. At the offset T-Junction turn right, along the main path and away from the trees, in the direction of a small enclosed plantation. Pass through the gap in the walls ahead, with the small plantation to your right, and descend the last few yards to the car park.

14. BURBAGE

A circular walk taking in Goyt's Moss and three of the main tributaries to the upper Goyt.

Distance: 5.5 miles (9km)

Allow: 2 hours 30 minutes

Maps: White Peak 1:25,000

How to get there

Follow the directions for route 11, then follow the road down the Goyt Valley to the car park at Goytsclough Quarry.

Refreshments: This route passes the Cat & Fiddle Inn on the Buxton – Macclesfield road.

From the car park at Goytsclough Quarry, the original site from which Pickfords removals started operations, turn right up the road towards Derbyshire Bridge. After a short distance cross the river to your left via the footbridge. From here a right turn will lead you quickly onto the main path that traverses Goyt's Moss. Walk alongside the River Goyt to where Berry Clough enters on your right. At this point follow the path along the side of Berry Clough, with bracken interspersed with the rough moorland grasses.

Cross a stream which enters from the left, then follow the path as it deviates from the banks of Berry Clough. The path now crosses another tributary with a sharp right turn, followed by a sharp left. After a few yards you pass a track coming in from your right, and continue onwards to the top of the rise. This is the southern end of Burbage Edge, with good views back down into the Goyt Valley. Cross the wall ahead, then move diagonally right towards the far end of the woodland.

Follow the wall around the corner of the woods then down to where the Cromford and High Peak Railway line joins a major path. Turn sharp right here, almost doubling back on yourself, then continue to a footpath

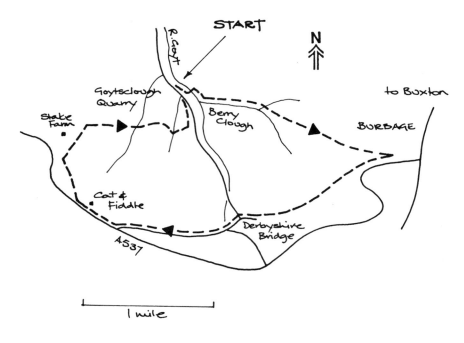

on your left. The path now climbs up the flanks of Axe Edge Moor, across open country. This is another good spot to see one of the region's summer visitors, the wheatear.

This member of the thrush family is a common visitor to the moors and heaths of northern England, and particularly the southern Pennines. Arriving in late March it is one of the earliest of the summer visitors, and is easily recognisable by its white rump. Both sexes display yellow breasts, but the male in spring is particularly attractive with its black, white and grey head pattern.

Wheatear

Care should be taken to stick to the paths as this species is ground nesting and therefore is easily disturbed by straying walkers. Continue down the track, keeping straight on as you pass several alternative paths to either side. The next turning comes at a T-junction by a wall, where a left turn drops you down onto the road. Follow the road steeply downhill to a junction, then turn left to rise again up to the Macclesfield road. A right turn at the road, opposite an AA telephone, will bring you to the Cat & Fiddle Inn – the country's second highest pub, at 1690ft. This is a pleasant sight on a cold, wet day, and being on several major footpath routes the management are quite used to ramblers and offer a warm welcome. On summer weekends it is sometimes possible to take a helicopter trip over the surrounding area, at a price.

From the Cat & Fiddle walk up the road towards Macclesfield, taking care as it is still a busy road, to a right hand turn just past the milepost. The path now climbs alongside a wall, which soon disappears, with Stake Farm below to your left. Once past the farm take a right hand turn to head down towards the plantations on Stake Side, the wall on your left providing a guide. The path meets the corner of the plantation, then turns right across another path. Cross Stake Clough and continue around the edge of the plantation to a wall. Once over this wall you enter the trees temporarily to meet Deep Clough. Climb the opposite bank of the stream, veering left, and continue round the bend to a path leading off sharply to the left. This path leads downhill to the roadway at the end of Goytsclough quarry, and your starting point.

15. SOLOMON'S TEMPLE

A short walk to one of Buxton's most visible landmarks, offering superb views over the town.

Distance: 4 miles (6.5km)

Allow: 1 hour 30 minutes

Maps: White Peak 1:25,000

How to get there

By car: Buxton is located on the A6 between Derby and Manchester, 12 miles west of Bakewell.

By bus: Buxton is well served by buses from Manchester, Nottingham, Derby and Sheffield. Summer services also run between the town and The Potteries.

By train: Buxton Station is at the end of the line to Manchester Piccadilly, and has an hourly service throughout the year.

Refreshments: the town has numerous pubs and cafés, with the market place providing the greatest range, including The Kings Head, Eagle, New Inn, Rising Sun and Cheshire Cheese.

The ideal starting point for this walk is the car park outside Poole's Cavern on the south side of the town. This is also the beginning of Buxton Country Park, and the walk is through a large part of the park.

From the far side of the car park a narrow opening in the wall leads into the obvious deciduous woodland ahead, and immediately starts to rise. At the first crossroads in the paths go straight ahead. As the path begins to move left and climb it divides the woodland into two halves, the lower being entirely deciduous, while the upper portion is a true mixed woodland exhibiting a variety of deciduous and coniferous trees with no apparent pattern.

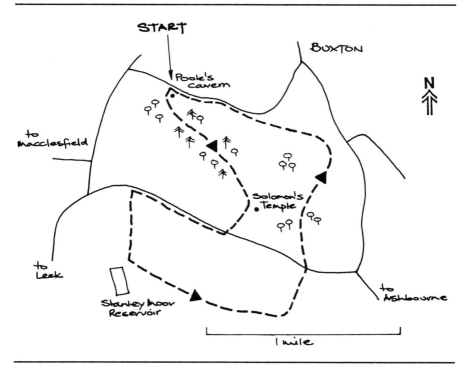

Four main trees dominate the deciduous sections of the woodland: sycamore, beech, ash and elm. Of these, only the sycamore provides a problem in maintenance, while the ash and elm, in particular, are simple to control. The major problem with the sycamore is its great ability to spread. Since its introduction some 500 years ago it has rapidly become the dominant species. With its large leaves, which come early in the year, it spreads a large shadow and prevents other species growing at ground level. In addition it tends to support only a minor number of insects, and therefore supports a smaller variety of birds.

As you approach a corner of two walls on your left, and a broken wall to your right, the path divides into three with the main branch heading left. At this point follow the central route, which heads directly for a small gap in the boundary wall. On exiting you are once more confronted by a choice of routes, and again the way onwards is straight ahead. The route now is simple to follow, with the landmark of Solomon's Temple being your target.

The temple, or Grinlow Tower as it is otherwise known, is possibly Buxton's most obvious attraction. The tower is actually a folly, conceived by a local farmer called Solomon Mycock in 1896 to give work to the local unemployed. Standing 440 ft above the town it gives superb views of the surrounding area. The rough ground surrounding the temple is actually the remains of a number of Neolithic tumuli, with relics of early human habitation of the area displayed in Buxton Museum.

Beyond the temple, the path heads steeply down the hill, crossing rough pasture on its way to the road below. At the road turn right, and continue for half a mile to the obvious path on your left. This path now heads directly across Stanley Moor, towards the reservoir. Be careful not to fall down one of the holes that dot Stanley Moor – they can be deep.

For many years this has been an extremely interesting, and frustrating, place for local cavers. The swallets here have been dye-tested to trace their water course, and a link has been proved with Poole's Cavern. Despite this link, and the possibility of creating a large system the connection is as far off as ever. The main swallets, Plunge Hole and Axe Hole, both have impressively large passages and entrance shafts, but are completely clogged with glacial mud which has so far proved an impenetrable barrier.

As you approach the corner of the small reservoir ahead, the path turns left before meeting a T-junction. Turn left at this junction, keeping the wall to your left, then bend to your right shortly after the gate ahead. From here the path, which is a wide track, heads towards the base of Countess Cliff, and completes a semi-circular turn around the high point of Stanley Moor before dropping very steeply to rejoin the road. On reaching the road, with steep climbs to either side, cross over and turn slightly left to reach the continuation on your right.

Yet again the path starts to rise, crossing a number of fields to reach the edge of a small wood just before Fern House. Pass the woodland on your right, and by following the wall on your right you can bypass the buildings of Fern House. Continue ahead till a path exits on your left, and follow this for a few yards to join a further path. A left turn here leads you in a straight line below High Plantation and Solomon's Temple. On your left is a steep path, leading back into the woods, which is obvious in winter due to its use as a toboggan run. Ignore this turning, and the corresponding continuation to your right, and continue ahead to the road. From this point it is a short walk up the road to your left to Poole's Cavern and your starting point.

In future years some of the recent development work carried out on the woodland should provide walkers with even more variety. To increase diversity and reduce the dominance of the sycamore a number of species have been planted throughout. Lime, rowan, oak, hazel, hornbeam, horse chestnut, hawthorn, holly and wild rose have all been introduced. This will also increase the available habitats for bird life, which is presently restricted to nesting in the artificial brashings spread throughout the woodland.

16. WILDBOARCLOUGH

A walk through open moors to Wildboarclough, then via Gradbach to the village of Danebridge, taking in the mixed woodland around Lud's Church.

Distance: 8 miles (13km)

Allow: 3 hours

Maps: White Peak 1:2500

How to get there

By car: The Wild Boar is on the A54 Buxton to Congleton, shortly after the Wildboarclough-Wincle crossroads.

By train: there is no railway station nearby.

By bus: no regular bus service operates nearby.

Refreshments: Crag Inn at Wildboarclough and the Rose and Crown and Wild Boar on the main road.

The route starts at the car park of the Wild Boar public house on the main Buxton to Congleton road. The interior decorating of the pub is interesting for its boar skin on the wall – wearing glasses. Although it is closed in the late afternoon the Wild Boar makes a perfect start and finish point, having a good choice of food as well as a nice pint of Robinsons.

Cross the field behind the pub to its far right corner, then cross into the next field with a wall on the right. Keep this wall to your right for the next two fields, then cross the wall with Hammerton Knowl farm ahead. The path now moves away from the wall to join the main track up to the farm. Turn right at the farm and go downhill towards to the Wildboarclough-Wincle road.

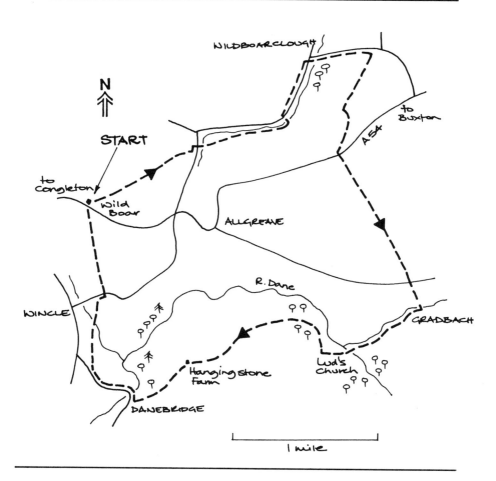

Turn left along the road, then after a few yards turn right onto open ground. The small stream ahead makes the ground softer and supports various species, including the soft rush.

The soft rush differs from the hard rush by its apparent glossy and smooth stalk. The flowers may be in either a loose cluster or a compact bunch, and it is a common plant in the acid soils of the Peak District.

After crossing the stream continue ahead to be joined by a wall on your left. Follow this wall to a T-junction, then turn left to skirt a small mixed wood on your right. Beyond the wood the path rejoins the small stream

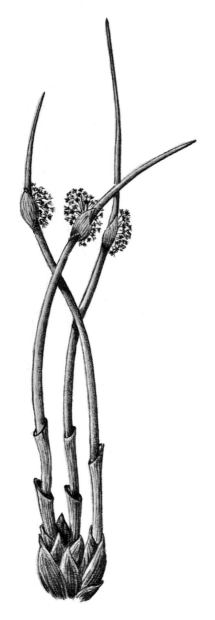

Soft Rush

from earlier in the route, which has become Clough Brook. Continue along the right hand bank of Clough Brook to meet a car park, just before Wildboarclough. At the car park join the road, and continue to the village, passing the Crag Inn to your left.

As you enter Wildboarclough take the road turning to your right, and walk up the steep slope ahead. To your left is Crag Hall at the top of the road, and the route on is directly opposite. Turn right, off the road, and walk alongside a narrow belt of mixed trees to Firs Farm. Beyond the farm, at the end of the trees, the path turns sharply to the right and briefly enters a small conifer plantation. Beyond the plantation walk across two fields diagonally right, then walk up to the Congleton road.

Cross the main road to join a large track heading south-east, and follow this for three quarters of a mile across open moorland to reach another road. Below to your right are Heild Rocks, Helmesley rocks and Allgreave, while you also pass a well on your right part way along the track. At the road, cross straight over to rejoin the path which descends to the River Dane at Gradbach. Cross the river by the footbridge, and turn right by the old mill (now a youth hostel). Now walk along beside the river towards the obvious plantation ahead. Cross the footbridge into Forest Wood and join the main path up to Lud's Church.

Turn right by Lud's Church to exit the woodland, and join a wall on your right. The route here is again a major track, and it rises slowly to join a T-junction. Turn right at the junction and descend past the Paddock to Hangingstone Farm. Pass through the farm and across the field behind to enter a rough mixed woodland with bracken on the fringes. The path now cuts downhill through the trees, and across a small stream, to emerge at Danebridge.

At Danebridge you again join the road, turning right to cross the river, then walk uphill towards Wincle. Just after the pub a path leaves to the right, which cuts across country past the small hamlet at Wincle to join Hog Clough. Cross Hog Clough and walk diagonally left across the field to join a further road. Turn right at the road, then almost immediately left at Hammerton Farm. The route now continues alongside the left hand wall as it crosses Hammerton Moss, again a perfect spot to study the soft rush. Shortly after the isolated trees to your left the path is joined by another from the left, and you reach the Congleton Road. Directly in front of you is the Wild Boar, and your starting point.

If timed right, and at the correct season this is a very enjoyable walk, covering a variety of habitats and walking terrain. Much of the route is through rough moorland, but sections of river walking and farmland give much needed variety. With the addition of the three mentioned pubs, and a further one just off the route at Danebridge, the route can be done in stages to amplify the different terrains. The bird life is particularly interesting as it changes from one habitat to another, with Gradbach and Wildboarclough being noteworthy for owls in particular.

17. FLASH

A short, but exposed, walk through rough moorland, passing close to the sources of the Dove and Manifold Rivers.

Distance: 4.5 miles (7km)

Allow: 1 hour 30 minutes

Maps: White Peak 1:25000

How to get there

By car: the village of Flash lies just off the main A53 Buxton to Leek road, at an altitude of 1550ft (470m).

By train: the nearest station is at Buxton, several miles away.

By bus: there is an irregular bus service between Buxton and Leek, with stops on the main road half a mile from the village. Other services operate seasonally and irregularly.

Refreshments: the nearest pub is the Rising Sun on the A53 near the Flash turning.

For ease of parking, this route starts at the Rising Sun on the main road. From the pub take the main road towards Leek, and turn down the first road to your right. As you reach the end of the buildings making up Flash village take a right turn up a small lane. After a few yards a path exits to the right across the fields. Follow this path, which rises slowly through the fields on the flank of Oliver Hill.

The moorland here, as in much of the area, is rough and consists of a small number of hardy species. One of the most common of these is bog cotton, or cotton grass. This is a short, creeping perennial which is particularly suited to the wet peaty soils of the Peak District. In May and June it displays small groups of hanging flower spikes, which change in July as the fruits come through. It is the long cottony hairs attached to this fruit that provide its name, along with its affinity to wet, boggy areas.

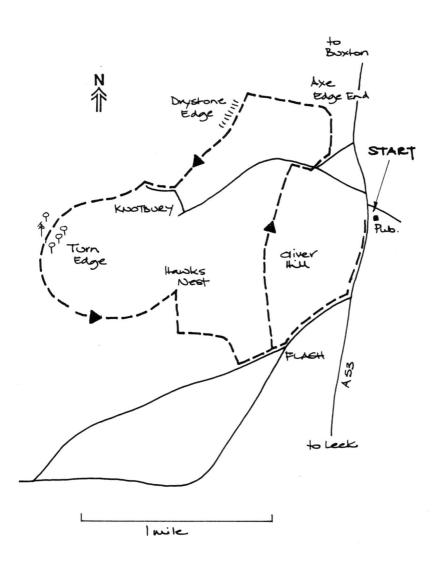

Bog Cotton

As you leave the hill top the wall to your left, which has provided a useful guide, disappears. Cross the next two fields diagonally to the left, then head across the large open area to join the road. A right turn onto the road is shortly followed by a left turn along the Hilltop road. Beyond Hilltop a minor road leads left to Axe Edge End and a junction of several footpaths. Take the left hand path where the road forks, then turn left at the path crossroads. You have now crossed into Derbyshire, but this is short lived as the path returns into Staffordshire at the wall ahead.

Cross the two streams ahead (the first one has a footbridge) and walk up to Drystone Edge and a T-junction. Left here takes you along the foot of Drystone Edge, with the wall on your right aiding navigation. As you approach Readyleech Green the path turns into a farm road. Turn right at the T-junction, then left at the end of the field on your left hand side. The track now descends alongside a wall (left) to Knotbury, and a minor road. Follow the road ahead to a footpath on the left, then cross the field in front. The drainage channel to your left leads across the moor, with the path alongside it. Just past the junction of the drainage channels the path curves to the left and heads into a small mixed wood.

As the path leaves the trees behind it turns into a small lane, and skirts the southern edge of Turn Edge. Follow this track round the hill till Hawk's Nest is just in front of you, and take the path on the right. Follow this path down to a tributary of the river Dane. At the footbridge you cross the stream, turn left and head steeply uphill through the fields. At the next T-junction turn right and follow the track down to the road. A left turn here leads steeply uphill to Flash, and the road back to your starting point.

18. GOYT VALLEY AND THREE SHIRE HEADS

A long, and arduous walk through the Goyt Valley then over Axe Edge Moor to Three Shire Heads, returning via the Cat & Fiddle. Mixed countryside throughout gives an ideal opportunity to study numerous species in relatively unspoilt surroundings.

Distance: 11.25 miles (18km)

Allow: 5 hours

Map: Peak District Touring Map, White Peak

How to get there

The starting point is a car park in the Goyt Valley, which is only accessible by car from Long Hill, half a mile north west of Buxton. Alternatively the walk may be joined from Buxton at Burbage.

By bus: service 198/199 half hourly from Buxton/Stockport; service 252 hourly from Manchester/Nottingham

By train: hourly service between Manchester Piccadilly to Buxton

Refreshments: there are numerous pubs in Buxton town centre. The Duke of York at Burbage and the Cat & Fiddle Inn are both on or close to the route.

The starting point for this walk is the car park at the north west corner of Errwood Reservoir. From the car park cross the old Roman Road, The Street, and follow the road ahead to the dam head. The embankment gives superb views of the Goyt Valley, with Fernilee Reservoir to the left and Errwood to the right. The number of bird species to be found in this area is almost limitless and includes mallard, kestrel, lapwing, dipper, tawny owl and pipit. Tufted duck, teal, black headed gull, goldeneye

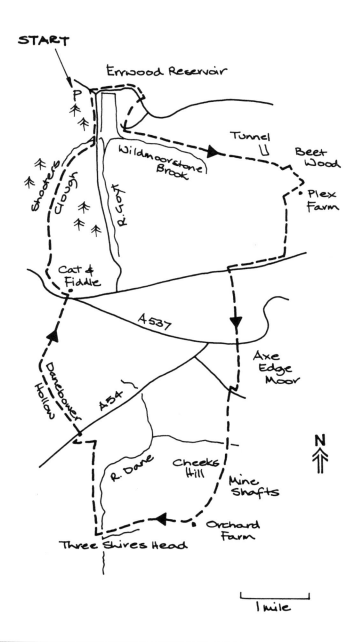

START

Errwood Reservoir

P

Tunnel

Beet Wood

Wildmoorstone Brook

Plex Farm

Shooters Clough

R. Goyt

Cat & Fiddle

A 537

Danebower Hollow

A 54

Axe Edge Moor

R. Dane

Cheeks Hill

Mine Shafts

N

Orchard Farm

Three Shires Head

1 mile

and great crested grebe are among the large variety of visitors found here during the colder months.

On leaving the dam head follow the road round to the left, then right, to join a track on the right hand side of a stiff climb. Continue along this track to a junction with Goyt's Lane, which now disappears below the waters of Errwood Reservoir, and continue straight across. The path then turns east to follow the left hand bank of Wildmoorstone Brook upstream. Continue along this path, crossing tributaries at three points, and a climb brings you to a blocked tunnel on the old Cromford and High Peak Railway. From here stick to the left hand side of the wall ahead, and climb steadily to the top of the rise till a right turn leads downhill to Beet Wood and a rough road via the ladder stile. Follow this road for 400 yards, then turn right again up a track leading past Plex Farm. At the head of the farm track a left turn brings you back to the disused railway line and a mile of easy walking to the old Buxton to Macclesfield turnpike. Once on the turnpike turn right, then take the second track on the left and into the moors. Continue south for half a mile, then cross the main road (A54) and emerge on Axe Edge Moor.

The country around Axe Edge is rough heather and ling moorland, where the peat can reach up to 12ft in depth. Care should be taken not to step into one of the many minor streams cutting through the peat. It is also worth remembering that you are now in the home of the red grouse. These, and other ground nesting species, may easily be disturbed by the unwary walker, especially during the breeding season. Signs are usually displayed in several places to advise of breeding and nesting seasons, so please take notice of them. By sticking to the obvious paths you should

Red Grouse

be able to avoid undue disturbance, and keep your feet dry at the same time.

Continue across Axe Edge Moor, staying to the right where it forks at Thatch Marsh. After a further 350 yards turn right onto the road, then immediately left to rejoin the moors and the path up to Cheeks Hill. On the following descent take care of the numerous abandoned mine shafts dotting the hillside. Keeping the disused quarry to your right continue downhill towards Orchard Farm, again staying right where the path forks. From Orchard Farm carry on straight ahead at the junction of two paths, then take the left hand route down to a tributary of the River Dane. The following half mile follows this tributary down to Three Shire Heads and the junction of Derbyshire with Cheshire and Staffordshire. This is a popular spot with walkers, particularly for its views south to the Roaches, and makes an ideal rest spot before the uphill slog back to the southern end of the Goyt Valley.

From Three Shire Heads turn right and follow the Dane upstream for a mile. Shortly after the path leaves the waterside near Reeve Edge Quarries a junction is reached where a left turn leads back to the A54. Follow the road to the north east for a few yards till a left turn is signposted up Danebower Hollow. This is a steady climb of a mile and a half that eventually leads you to the door of the Cat & Fiddle Inn, at 1690ft the second highest pub in England, and a very welcome sight.

Having left the hardest part of the walk behind the route now follows the main road towards Macclesfield for a few yards to an obvious turning on your right. Shortly after the milestone a further right is taken, then continue over a cross roads in the paths, and past the main track which heads of left to Shining Tor. From this point a pleasant downhill ramble alongside a mixed plantation leads to Shooter's Clough, and on downwards to the southern end of Errwood Reservoir. The last half mile is along the road, with the ruins of Errwood Hall to your left and the reservoir on your right, to return to your start point.

With such variations in altitude and exposure along the route it is interesting to note the change in plant species. In the early part of the walk the beech is the dominant tree, with grass lining the banks. As you progress towards Burbage the grasses change from the introduced varieties best suited to a managed site into the natural fescues found throughout the Peak. Once onto Axe Edge Moor the grasses give way to full scale heather. From the Cat & Fiddle heather is mixed with bilberry and crowberry, with a multitude of smaller wild species. As you progress back down into the Goyt spruce plantations take precedence over everything else, before giving way to natural Scot's Pine. Each of these species plays host to various birds, which change between coniferous plantation, deciduous and mixed woodland and open moor, in addition to those already mentioned which visit the open waters of the twin reservoirs.

For those looking for a more strenuous ending to the walk, with expansive views to the west, the path up to Shining Tor may be taken. From Shining Tor the ridge heads north to Pym's Chair, where a left turn leads down The Street between Sitka spruce plantations to the car park.

The Cat and Fiddle

Manifold and Dove Valleys

The twin rivers of the Manifold and Dove, rising from the moors of Axe Edge, are a total contrast from the walking of the two previous areas. Leaving the gritstone behind they flow south into the limestone, cutting deep into the 1000ft high plateau on their way. In some places they have provided wide valleys used for sheep and dairy grazing; in other places they are evident by the deep tree-lined gorges and steep cliff faces.

Poets' Rivers

Of the two rivers the Dove is undoubtedly the most popular, with its lower reaches attracting millions of visitors each year. Much of its popularity is due to the work of Charles Cotton and Izaak Walton, whose 17th century treatise "The Compleat Angler" introduced many to the beauty of the Dove and its fishing. The river has also attracted the attention of such noteable people as Ruskin, Byron and Tennyson, while prior to the advent of the motor car it attracted three daily horse and carriage tours from Buxton.

Award Winning Cheese

Hartington is the centre for studying the upper reaches of the Dove. The village is probably best known for its cheese factory which, being a quarter of a mile inside the county boundary, is allowed to make Stilton. True Stilton can only be made in the counties of Leicestershire, Nottinghamshire and Derbyshire, and the Hartington factory is regularly amongst the prize winners at cheese shows around the world.

Abandoned Lead Mines

The countryside to the north of Hartington is a mixture of natural and man made, with traditional stone walls dividing the fields much as they have for hundreds of years. The area was also extremely important as a lead mining centre in the 18th and 19th centuries. Since the decline of the industry many of the buildings associated with it have disappeared, but other remains dot the landscape and also serve a new purpose. Many of the mineral veins, called rakes, are still visible by the lines of trees planted on old spoil heaps. The land around the lead mines became so polluted and unworkable to farmers that they would only support narrow bands of trees. These now provide protection from the possibility of losing livestock down abandoned shafts, and useful windbreaks for sheltering herds. This is particularly important in such an exposed area where the wind tears across the plateau.

Site of Special Scientific Interest (S.S.S.I.)

To the south of Hartington the river course has lost much of its natural state. Weirs have been built across the river in several places to slow it down and to oxygenate the water for its superb stock of brown trout and grayling. Yew, alder, ash and beech line the valley and provide rich habitats for a wide variety of birds, while water figwort, water mint and yellow flag populate the riverside. As the river flows towards the vilage of Ilam it forms the county boundary of Staffordshire and Derbyshire, and includes an S.S.S.I. on its west bank due to its ecology.

Heron and Kingfisher

Though access is restricted the ash and beech woodlands combine well with the towering limestone cliffs and add to the visual pleasure of what has long been known as Derbyshire's most scenic dale. The sight of birds such as the heron, dipper, mallard and occasional kingfisher add to the effect and help entice ornithologists to join the ramblers. At its southern end, near the vilage of Ilam, the Dove joins another of the area's most scenic dales where it meets the River Manifold.

Ilam Hall

Ilam is possibly the most seasonally over-populated village in the western Peak, being the main centre for exploring both rivers. The Peak Park Joint Planning Board, in combination with the National Trust, have built a car and coach park for the vast number of annual visitors, along with extending the toilet block for walkers' convenience. Ilam Hall is a National Trust owned property which includes a tea room, camping and caravan site and youth hostel, along with an information centre and shop. Other nearby facilities include the Izaak Walton Hotel and a telephone, making Ilam an ideal centre for visiting the Dove and Manifold.

Copper Mines

The Manifold rises within half a mile of the Dove and follows a roughly parallel course for much of its length. From Axe Edge it flows south-east around Hollinsclough Moor to the village of Longnor, then south to Hulme End. Just beyond Hulme End its course is interupted by Ecton Hill, the site of some interesting old copper mines, and Wetton Hill. From Wettonmill to Beeston Tor, and the junction with the River Hamps, the valley is extremely steep sided and heavily wooded to either side, though a good path exists on its east flank.

Beyond Beeston Tor the valley widens considerably and the river takes a more mature, meandering course through ash and beech woods down to Ilam. The largest difference between the Manifold and the Dove is the size of the valleys they create, with the Manifold Valley reaching up to half a mile in width. Though similar in flora and fauna the Manifold is well worth a visit as it offers many of the delights of the Dove without the problems of overcrowding associated with the latter.

19. PILSBURY

A short walk giving two differing views of the upper Dove Valley.

Distance: 4 miles (6.5km)

Allow: 2 hours

Maps: White Peak 1:25000

How to get there

By car: Hartington village lies on the B5054, just off the A515 Buxton to Ashbourne Road. From the Potteries take the A52 or A53 to the A523, then turn onto the B5054.

By train: there is no railway station nearby.

By bus: various services operate, most of which vary in regularity depending on the season. Ashbourne, Leek and Buxton are all possible departure points.

Refreshments: refreshments are available at Hartington.

From Hartington Market Place take the road north towards Pilsbury, climbing steeply as you leave the village. After half a mile take the footpath on your left which remains level as you move north above the river.After crossing three fields Bank Top Farm appears below you to the left, and a wall appears on your right. Follow this wall, remaining on a level course, as you pass through remnants of the ancient woodlands which once covered much of the area.

As you reach a cross roads in the paths, evidence of the area's former importance as a lead mining centre becomes apparent, with both shafts and an adit to your left. Adits were driven as horizontal tunnels to aid drainage and recovery of the ore. Water was often a problem in the lower reaches of the mines, yet as ore was worked from the upper levels it was necessary to exploit these lower levels. By driving a level from

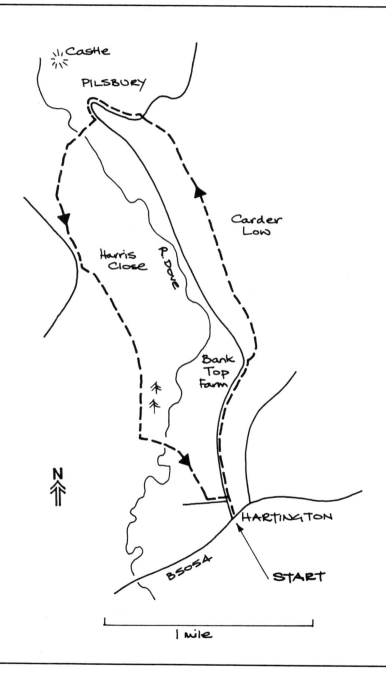

Castle

PILSBURY

Carder
Low

Harris
Close

P. Dove

Bank
Top
Farm

N

HARTINGTON

B5054

START

1 mile

lower down the hillside it was possible to take water away from the mine workings, and it is these drainage adits that appear in the hillsides around Hartington and other mining centres.

Go directly ahead at the cross roads, and cross another field. The path now deviates to the right, with a minor path to the left, cutting the corner of the next field. As you approach the tree to your right, take the track on your left. The track moves downhill to run alongside a wall on the left, then bends to join the road into Pilsbury. At the road walk straight on, and into the village.

Beyond Pilsbury turn right, off the road, and continue down a wide green lane to cross the River Dove. The footbridge leads to an obvious track, a stile and a gate. Take the stile into the next field and walk uphill to another stile in the uneven drystone wall. Pass round the gully and use the next stile to your right. Continue uphill to the next stile, which is located just to the left of the buildings. Continue ahead to where a stile part way along the hedgerow leads once more to a road.

Turn left, then left again to give access to Harris Close Farm, where a path leads between the buildings and a wall (right) to the fields. Keep the wall on your right as you pass through four fields, the first two with stiles and gates, the last two with stiles only. Continue ahead through the next field, dropping down to another stile, then rejoin the wall on your right. Keeping to the top of the bank, walk on to enter a plantation followed by a wood. The farm track ahead leads downhill between bushes to a road. Turn left off the road at the stile and gate, then carry on down to cross the Dove by way of the bridge. Turn right beyond the bridge, then take the stile, followed quickly by three further stiles. Aim for the left hand side of the buildings ahead, then cross the stile in the hedge. The hedge leads to a further stile and road. Turn left along the road to return to Hartington.

20. SHEEN

A medium distance walk crossing the ridge dividing the Manifold and Dove Valleys before returning to Hartington along the eastern edge of upper Dovedale.

Distance: 6 miles (9.5km)

Allow: 2 hours 30 minutes

Maps: White Peak 1:25000

How to get there

By car: Hartington village lies on the B5054, just off the A515 Buxton to Ashbourne Road. From the Potteries take the A52 or A53 to the A523, then turn onto the B5054.

By train: there is no railway station nearby.

By bus: various services operate, most of which vary in regularity depending on the season. Ashbourne, Leek and Buxton are all possible departure points.

Refreshments: refreshments are available at Hartington.

From Hartington take the road out of the village in the direction of Hulme End. As you approach the end of the houses on the right, before the police station/house, a footpath leads right between the buildings. Follow this path into the open country, and across six parallel fields. At the far end of the last field you encounter the river, and the road again. Turn right along the road for a few yards, then right again to ascend the hill up to Banktop Farm. The ridge to your right is the dividing line between the Manifold and Dove Valleys, and is tree lined throughout most of its length.

At Banktop turn right, between the buildings, and onwards to the road. Turn right at the road and continue towards Townend. Continue

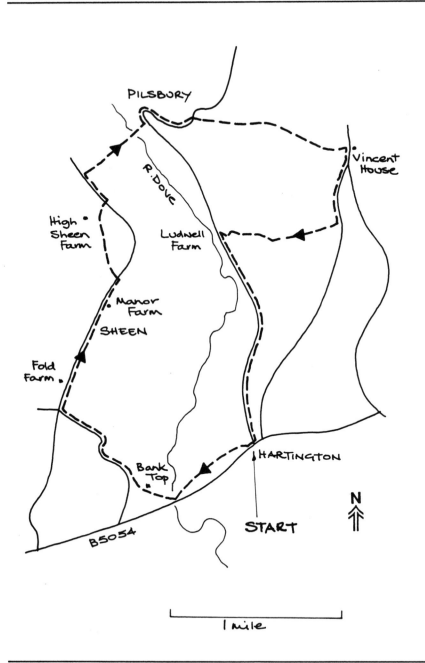

PILSBURY

Vincent
House

R. DOVE

High
Sheen
Farm

Ludwell
Farm

Manor
Farm

SHEEN

Fold
Farm

Bank
Top

HARTINGTON

START

N

B5054

1 mile

through Townend, where a right turn takes you onto the road to Longnor. Pass Fold Farm and continue on to the small village of Sheen. The road now continues past Manor Farm to a footpath on your left, which is taken across the fields. Cross the minor stream, just beyond the first wall, then traverse the next field diagonally right. The third field leads to the right of High Sheen Farm, and turns right by the side of a spring, where the wall on your left guides you to the road.

Once at the road turn left, with trees to your right, then take the track right at the end of the next field on that side. This track leads around an isolated tree, then straightens up to pass to the right of Broadmeadow Hall and so into Pilsbury. Pass through Pilsbury, and shortly after a left hand bend two paths turn off to the left. Ignore the first path (part of route 19), but take the second path to a cross roads. Go straight ahead at this cross roads and aim for the corner of the walls in front of you. Pass this corner and continue into the next field, with a small pond to your right, before the path curves right. Walk in a straight line across the next two fields, then move sharply left towards Vincent House, the obvious building in front.

Directly in front of Vincent House, turn right at the road. As the road forks take the right hand branch as far as a footpath leading off right. This path leads to the corner of the field, and then crosses to leave the wall on your right. Walk straight ahead as you pass through three consecutive fields, then take a wildly curving path across the next field, eventually reaching the far right corner. Just beyond the next wall you reach a cross roads, as in route 19, where you cross directly ahead. Extreme care should be taken here due to the number of abandoned mine shafts. The path meanders through two further fields to join the main Pilsbury to Hartington Road.

Turn left along this road, which is gated at the far end, opposite Ludwell Farm. The road now passes below the eastern ridge of upper Dovedale to Bank Top Farm. Continue down this road as it passes over a cattle grid and on past Moat Hall. The road now heads into Hartington via a gate, the garage and duckpond.

21. BERESFORD DALE

A short walk to the west of Hartington, finishing in a walk up one of the most scenic parts of Dovedale.

Distance: 3.25 miles (5km)

Allow: 1 hour 45 minutes

Maps: White Peak 1:25000

How to get there

By car: Hartington village lies on the B5054, just off the A515 Buxton to Ashbourne Road. From the Potteries take the A52 or A53 to the A523, then turn onto the B5054.

By train: there is no railway station nearby.

By bus: various services operate, most of which vary in regularity depending on the season. Ashbourne, Leek and Buxton are all possible departure points.

Refreshments: refreshments are available at Hartington.

From Hartington take the road out of the village in the direction of Hulme End. As you approach the end of the houses on the right, before the police station/house, a footpath leads right between the buildings. Follow this path into the open country, and across six parallel fields. At the far end of the last field you encounter the river, and the road again.

Turn right onto the road, then take the second path on your left. Continue south through the field, crossing a feeder to the Dove just beyond the first wall, and aim for the farmhouse ahead. As you approach Lower Hurst the path forks, but continue on the left fork to reach the farm itself. Beyond the farm the path becomes a wide track, which instantly divides. Take the left hand branch to a gap in the obvious thin lines of trees, and once through the gap turn right. The path

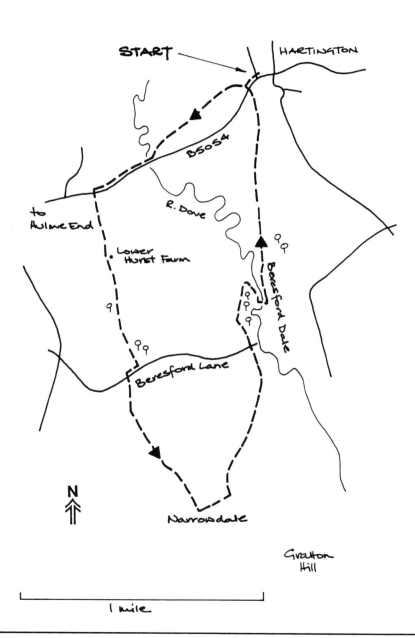

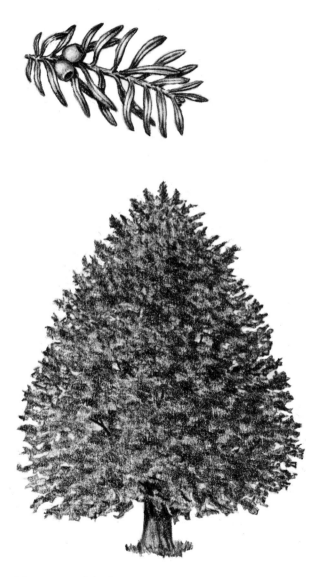

Yew tree and leaf

now runs south, with the trees to your right. After a gap of a single field you meet another line of trees, though this time to your left beyond a wall. Pass these trees to reach Beresford Lane, where you turn right onto the road.

Take the next path on your left, which crosses a narrow field, then continue diagonally right to meet the main track to Narrowdale. Ahead of you is Gratton Hill, while to the right is Wetton Hill and to the left is Wolfscote Hill. Each of these hills shows evidence of the long term habitation of this area, all being crowned by tumuli. At Narrowdale take the obvious track to your left which leads quickly to a T-junction, and a further left turn. The track now skirts the base of

Gratton Hill, heading back towards the river. Where the path forks take the left hand branch to rejoin Beresford Lane.

Cross the lane and follow the path north as it passes alongside trees to your right. Pass Beresford Cottage to your left, then turn immediately to the right, keeping to the edge of the woods. To the left lie the ruins of Beresford Hall, where Charles Cotton was born, and deep in the trees ahead is the fishing temple built by Cotton and Izaak Walton. The trees here are alder and yew, the natural species for the limestone dales. Unfortunately the woods are not accessible, but even from the edges the steep wooded cliffs give an insight into how the southern end of the peak may have been without human intervention.

The yew is an immensely long-lived tree, identifiable by its flaking reddish bark and heavily buttressed trunk. Male and female flowers occur on separate trees, and it is the female trees which exhibit the characteristic red fruit. The yew is particularly well adapted for survival in the limestone gorges, having the ability to grow on exposed cliffs and still prosper in shady areas. Their greatest advantage in the modern age, however, is their longevity and adaptability. In areas where species such as the sycamore have started to dominate, the yew remains.

At the far end of the woods the path hairpins back to a footbridge. Here you cross back into Derbyshire, and looking to your right the views are dominated by towering cliffs and alder trees. One suggestion for the appearance of Dovedale is that the whole of the valley from here southwards is in fact the collapsed remains of an enormous cave system running down to Ilam. Whatever the reason for its existence, the cliffs make an impressive sight. Once over the bridge follow the path to your left, along the tree-lined banks of the river. The path eventually moves away from the river to the right. Keep the wall on your left as you head into open country, and continue uninterrupted to emerge once more in Hartington.

22. BIGGIN DALE

A circular route south along a dry limestone valley, then back up
Dovedale to Hartington.

Distance: 5.5 miles (9km)

Allow: 2 hours 30 minutes

Maps: White Peak 1:25000

How to get there

By car: Hartington village lies on the B5054, just off the A515 Buxton to
Ashbourne Road. From the Potteries take the A52 or A53 to the A523,
then turn onto the B5054.

By train: there is no railway station nearby.

By bus: various services operate, most of which vary in regularity
depending on the season. Ashbourne, Leek and Buxton are all possible
departure points.

Refreshments: refreshments are available at Hartington.

From Hartington take the the B5054 towards Ashbourne to the War
Memorial. Turn right here and climb steeply to a large house. This is
Hartington Hall, built in 1611 as a manor house, now used as a youth
hostel. Continue with the line of trees to your right, and where they end
take a right turn up a stony track. You now climb steadily to the top of
the hill, where the view opens out dramatically. To your right is
Wolfscote Hill, with the Dove running to its right down Wolfscote Dale.
To the left of Wolfscote Hill lies Biggin Dale, the dry valley that is your
eventual target.

At this point continue straight ahead, passing several turnings, to reach
the buildings at Dale End. At the road bear right, passing a bungalow on
the right. Take the stile by the second gate on your right to enter Biggin

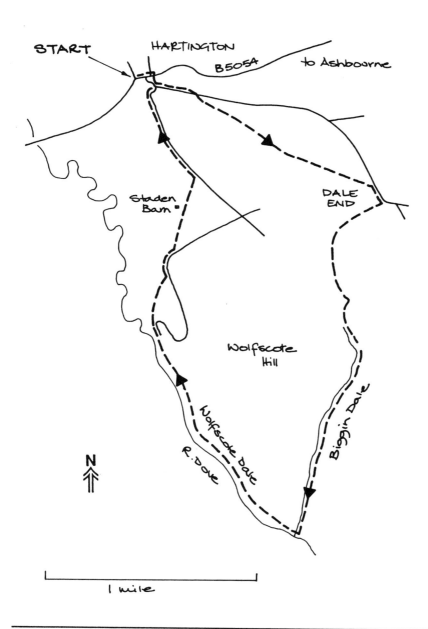

Dale, with a small sewage works to your right. Biggin Dale is totally dry in its upper reaches, and the lower reaches are only wet in winter, with a small stream running to join the Dove at Wolfscote Dale.

Continue down Biggin Dale, with yew trees to either side, to where a path joins from the right. Continue left here, but as the path bends to the left take a right turn. The trees are now on the right hand side and the ground has become rougher, with a multitude of wild plants amongst the grass. Where grass replaces woodland in the limestone dales the ground supports a large variety of grasses and sedges, along with a number of flowering plants. Lady's mantle, harebell, purging flax, violets, thyme and orchids may all be found on the more level ground, while the cliffs and screes are full of plants such as dark red helleborine, bloody crane'sbill and melancholy thistle.

Common Spotted Orchid

The common spotted orchid is England's most common orchid. It has rather narrow, dark-spotted leaves on short stems. The flowers are pink, or occasionally white marked with dull purple, and measure 10mm across the three lobed lip. It should be remembered that orchids have been collected to the point where species such as the lady's slipper are now almost extinct, so please leave the flowers where they look best – in the ground.

The path continues through Biggin Dale to join the lower part of Wolfscote Dale at Peasland Rocks. Turn right, upstream, and walk beside the river as it passes over several weirs. These have been built to provide more oxygenated water for the fish which stock the Dove, and to reduce the water speed. After the sixth set of weirs you reach a footbridge to your left crossing the county boundary into Staffordshire. Ignore this bridge, but turn directly to your right onto a wide track. Go straight ahead at the cross roads, and continue to a minor road where you turn left. Follow this road round a sharp left hand bend and onwards past Staden Barn to Reynards Lane. Turn left along Reynards Lane and follow the road on into Hartington.

23. DALEHEAD

A circular route from Biggin taking in a large portion of the upper Dove, combining open pasture with tree lined river paths.

Distance: 6 miles (9.5km)

Allow: 2 hours 30 minutes

Maps: White Peak 1:25000

How to get there

By car: Hartington village lies on the B5054, just off the A515 Buxton to Ashbourne Road. From the Potteries take the A52 or A53 to the A523, then turn onto the B5054. Biggin lies 2 miles south-east of Hartington.

By train: there is no railway station nearby.

By bus: various services operate, most of which vary in regularity depending on the season. Ashbourne, Leek and Buxton are all possible departure points.

Refreshments: refreshments are available at Hartington

The route starts at Dalehead, south west of Biggin, but may be joined at Coldeaton if parking is easier. To reach Dalehead from Biggin village take the road towards Hartington, turning left at Dale End by the modern bungalow. This road leads directly to Dalehead.

From Dalehead follow Liffs Road south, rising as you go. To your left the land is divided into small neat fields by the drystone walls which followed the enclosures of the 18th and 19th centuries. To your right the land is still enclosed but the fields are much larger, and give way after a short distance to the remains of an old quarry. Beyond Back Lane (left) the left hand side takes on a more hillocky nature with the remains of old lead mines and an old quarry on the northern flank of Johnson's Knoll.

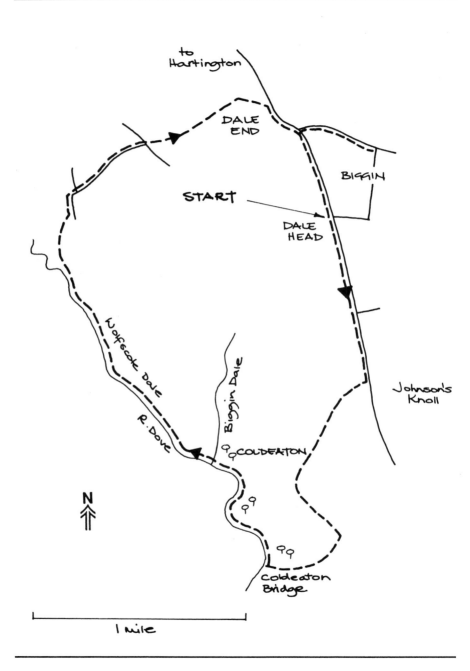

At the top of the hill take the path to your left which heads downhill towards Coldeaton. The path is a wide track, passing another abandoned quarry to your right just before a track heads off right. Ignore this track, but continue down to Coldeaton, passing an area of scrub on your left shortly before reaching the buildings. Navigate your way between the buildings to a path leading left alongside a wall (left). This short path continues downhill to where a sharp S bend leads to a T-junction.

At the junction turn right with mixed woodlands ahead of you on the right hand side. The path now enters a steep side valley, afforested on its northern (right) flank. Continue down the dale, keeping to the edge of the trees, and join the Dove valley. As you join the main river valley turn right to Coldeaton Bridge, but ignore the footbridge and continue

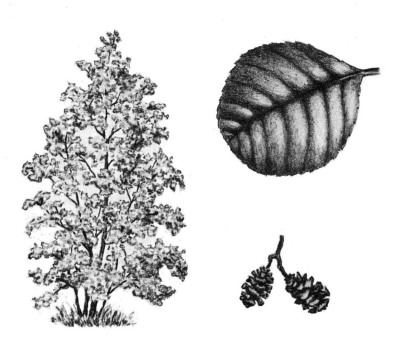

Alder – top - leaf structure, bottom - fruit

along the bank of the river. The river banks here are ideal ground for the alder tree, one of the major pioneering trees in colonising new ground.

The alder has a regular, conical crown when in its early years, but becomes more open and irregular as it matures. The rounded leaves resemble the hazel, but may be differentiated by the slightly indented tip. The catkins are particularly interesting, with the male catkin being purple and yellow and the female hardening from small purple-brown catkins to a hard, dark brown cone.

The footpath stays on the right hand bank of the river, between the water and the trees, as it continues north. As you approach the junction of Biggin Dale and Wolfscote Dale you pass a series of stepping stones through the river, and a cave to your right. As you pass the weir you are joined by the path from Biggin Dale (right), opposite Peasland Rocks. Turn right, upstream, and walk beside the river as it passes over several weirs. After the sixth set of weirs you reach a footbridge to your left crossing the county boundary into Staffordshire. Ignore this bridge, but turn directly to your right onto a wide track. Go straight ahead at the cross roads, and continue to a minor road where you turn left. Follow this road round to where a track leads straight ahead as the road turns sharp left.

Follow this track to a crossroads with a road leading off left and tracks ahead and right. Take the track ahead, then right at the next crossroads to walk down to Dale End. From here Biggin is a short walk down the next turning to the left, or continue right to return to Dalehead.

24. PARWICH

A walk over the limestone plateau, linking Parwich with Tissington.

Distance: 7.5 miles (12km)

Allow: 2 hours 30 minutes

Maps: White Peak 1:25000

How to get there

By car: Parwich lies 15 miles south of Buxton on the A515 Buxton to Ashbourne road, 6 miles north of Ashbourne.

By train: no suitable stations in the vicinity.

By bus: various services operate, most of which vary in regularity depending on the season. Ashbourne, Leek and Buxton are all possible departure points.

Refreshments: refreshments are available at Parwich and Tissington.

This walk starts from the centre of Parwich, and leaves the village to the west along Dam Lane. As the road bends to the right take the footpath on the left hand side into the ancient system of drystone wall enclosed fields. The first three quarters of a mile consists of a westerly walk across meadows, going straight ahead at a crossroads and ignoring the only footpath which exits to the left.

As you approach Parwich Lees the path goes between an isolated area of trees, before meeting a wide track where a right turn leads onto the road. Turn right along Dam Lane, towards Parwich, for a few yards till you meet a track heading off to your left. Turn left at the crossroads, behind Parwich Lees and parallel to the road. After a short climb the path leads over level ground before dropping into Alsop En Le Dale.

Place names such as Alsop En Le Dale and Chapel-en-le-Frith show evidence of the times when the great forest clearings were started. The

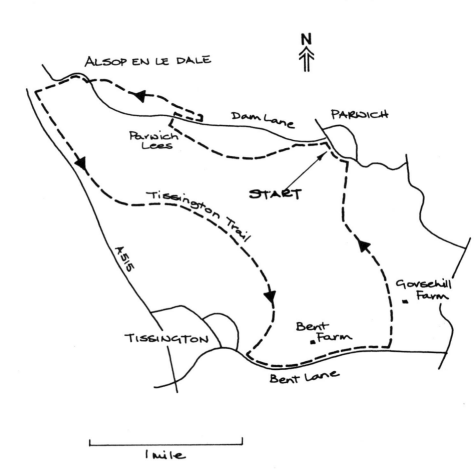

whole of this area was formerly a forest, but with the Norman conquest clearing of the woodland started as the area sprouted settlements. At Pilsbury, north of Hartington, the remains of the Norman civilisation are well shown by the ruins of a motte and bailey castle. Castleton, north of Buxton also contains the remains of a stone built castle dating from the same era. Prior to the Norman period the area had neolithic, then Roman, and then Anglo-Saxon settlements, with the Romans in particular being interested in the easily accessible deposits of lead. These periods, however, did not bring the same level of tree felling, or permanent change to the countryside.

Walk through the hamlet of Alsop En Le Dale to a path on the left, at the crown of a right hand bend. Follow this path uphill to join the Tissington Trail. This is one of three major disused railway lines converted into cycling and walking trails. The Monsal Trail runs from near Buxton to Bakewell in the central Peak, whilst the High Peak and Tissington Trails cover the area between Buxton and Ashbourne.

The Tissington Trail now forms your route into Tissington, passing the New Inns Hotel to the right, and running parallel to the A515 for the first half mile. The route is easy to follow as it curves left, then right, to arrive just south of Tissington. From Tissington take the road leading out to the east, Bent Lane, and follow it for three quarters of a mile past Bent Farm. The road now starts to drop and you pass one path leading off left, before taking the second left downhill across the plateau.

Pass Gorsehill Farm to your right before dropping to Bletch Brook. Cross the stream and continue, now uphill, to where the path forks. Take the left hand route, which rapidly gets steeper, using Bletch Brook below to your left as a guide. The path runs parallel to the stream for half a mile, passing two turnings to your right before reaching a T-junction. Turn right at the junction and a short walk back into Parwich.

25. TISSINGTON

A circular route using the Tissington Trail to reach Thorpe near the southern end of the Dove, returning across the limestone plateau to enter Tissington from the west.

Distance: 3.5 miles (5.5km)

Allow: 1 hour 15 minutes

Maps: White Peak 1:25000

How to get there

By car: Tissington lies just of the A515 Buxton to Ashbourne road 4 miles north of Ahbourne.

By train: there are no railway stations nearby.

By bus: intermittent services operate, seasonally from Buxton and Ashbourne.

Refreshments: refreshments are available at Tissington.

Tissington village has become famous throughout the Peak as the traditional site of the first well dressing each year. The well dressing here was first recorded in 1758, and always takes place on Ascension Day. Other interesting sights in Tissington include the Hall, which is rarely open to the public, and a fine church.

The route starts from the car park on the Tissington Trail. Pass the toilet block and continue south along the trail towards Ashbourne, crossing over the A515 then under a blue brick bridge. The cutting here is an important nature reserve under the management of the Derbyshire Wildlife Trust. The main reason for its existance is a wide variety of wild flowers. Lady's mantle, harebell, purging flax, violets, thyme and orchids may all be found, along with the rich yellow rockrose, milkwort and meadow rue.

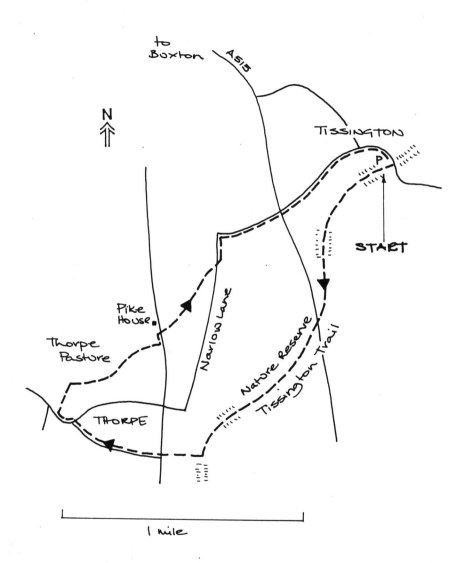

Milkwort

The milkwort is a common grassland perennial which comes in a variety of colours. Here it is mainly found as a short woody stemmed plant whose leaves decrease in size up the stem. The flowers are of an unusual shape and come in various colours – blue, white, purplish pink, and purple tipped with pink.

Beyond the cutting you arrive at the former Thorpe Cloud railway station. Go on past the station for 100 yards to a footpath signposted Thorpe and Dovedale on your right hand side. Head towards the large house ahead and pass through a double stile. A further single stile leads to the road, which you cross to walk past The Firs and Broadlow Ash Farm. Now drop down into Thorpe village, where a left turn leads onto the main road. Turn right by the telephone box and continue onto Thorpe Pastures, an area of common land where grazing rights are held in common by all. It is noticeable that the common, regular walls which divide so much of the area are missing here.

Head right across the pasture, aiming for Pike House. As you approach Pike House the path deviates to your right to join Spend Lane. Turn left along this lane, then right after a few yards across four fields to join Narlow Lane by the side of a disused quarry. Turn left along the road and follow it round a sharp right hand bend, now called Washbrook Lane. The road now leads to a crossroads with the A515, where you go straight ahead (caution! this is an extremely busy road and is hazardous to cross). The road now leads directly into Tissington, passing the grounds of Tissington Hall on your left.

26. THORPE

A walk from Thorpe up Dovedale, returning across the plateau between Dovedale and Tissington.

Distance: 5.5 miles (9km)

Allow: 2 hours 30 minutes

Maps: White Peak 1:25000

How to get there

By car: Thorpe lies 2 miles to the west of the A515 Buxton to Ashbourne road 3 miles north of Ashbourne.

By train: there are no suitable stations nearby.

By bus: intermittent services operate seasonally from Buxton and Ashbourne.

Refreshments: refreshments are available in Thorpe.

From Thorpe take the route up the bank of Hamston Hill onto Thorpe Pastures. By the side of a disused quarry (right) take the path up Lin Dale. On your way up Hamston Hill keep your eyes open for a red flag which is a warning indicator of firing at the nearby rifle range. Pass to the right of the imposing Thorpe Cloud, with a well to your left as you rise towards Dovedale. Pass to the left of the trees as the path curves left, and join the main Dovedale path at a T-junction.

Turn right at this junction to enter the most popular part of Dovedale. The path has been improved over recent years due to the large volume of traffic, particularly in summer, and the going is considerably easier than in former times. The path goes upstream along the west bank of the Dove and passes many of the most well known, and photogenic, landmarks of Dovedale. The first of these landmarks is Dovedale Castle on the opposite bank of the river, visible as you ascend a small hill

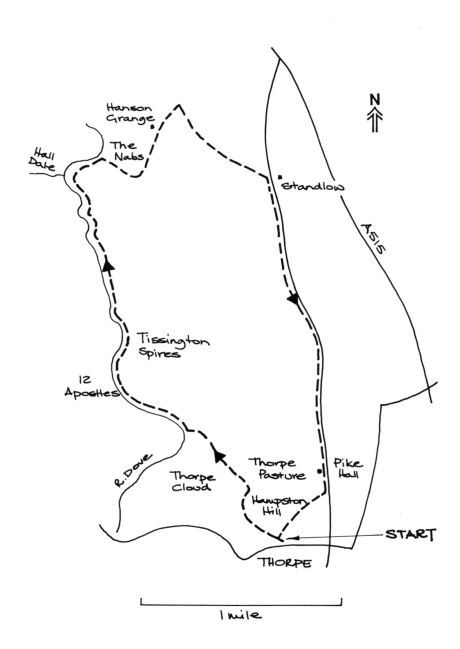

called Sharplow Rise.

After the crag of Dovedale Castles come the pinnacles of the Twelve Apostles, again on the opposite side. The hill you have climbed to view the Twelve Apostles is one of many in the Peak to carry the name Lovers' Leap. The story behind this Lovers' Leap relates to a suicide pact between two lovers; like so many others, it proved unsuccessful. Continue upstream through a double stile to the next landmark, Tissington Spires, on your right. Opposite is Jacob's Ladder, again a popular name throughout limestone districts.

Beyond Tissington Spires the valley narrows again and you pass the remains of an old pumping house formerly used by farmers to transfer water to the plateau above. As limestone is so porous water collection has long been a major problem. In the days before large scale reservoirs were available the habit was to build a circular pond in fields to collect the water, a common sight throughout the Peak, and known as dewponds. The alternative was to pump water from a nearby river, as seen here and further up the valley at Nabs Dale.

Opposite the old pumping station is another rock formation, called Dovedale Church, which is followed after 200 yards by a large natural arch high up to your right. At the far end of this is Reynard's Cave, a popular spot with photographers and artists. Beyond this lies a section of wooden boardwalk through The Narrows and a further double stile leading to Lion's Head Rock. Adjacent to Lion's Head Rock is a plaque to one of the founders of the move to buy the land for the National Trust – F.A.Holmes.

The next landmarks are Ilam Rock, on the opposite bank, and Pickering Tor to your right. At this point Dovedale continues ahead, upstream, while Hall Dale enters on the opposite side. As you reach a series of caves, Dove Holes, you arrive at a path signposted Alsop-en-le-Dale and a steep climb to your right. Climb up Nabs Dale, passing The Nabs to your left as the path curves towards Hanson Grange. Pass to the left of the buildings and take a track to the right. Follow this for a few yards to a five way junction where you turn sharp right.

The track now heads south east to join Gag Lane (or Gagg Lane) opposite Standlow. Follow the lane towards Thorpe, with a quarry high up to your right after half a mile. Hollington Barn is the next building to your right and is followed by more abandoned quarries on the same side. Just past a further quarry, close to the roadside on your right, is Pike House. 100 yards further on a path leads right, signposted, to Thorpe. The narrow squeezer leads to two further examples of this type of stile. After the third squeezer turn left and follow the stream down across the lower section of Thorpe Pastures and your starting point at Thorpe village.

27. ILAM

A circular route from Ilam to the head of Hall Dale, then down Dovedale to the Izaak Walton Hotel and so back to the popular centre for exploring both the Dove and Manifold.

Distance: 4.5 miles (7km)

Allow: 2 hours

Maps: White Peak 1:25000

How to get there

By car: Ilam lies to the west of the A515 Buxton to Ashbourne road 3 miles north of Ashbourne.

By train: there are no suitable stations nearby.

By bus: intermittent services operate, seasonally from Buxton and Ashbourne.

Refreshments: Refreshments are available at the Izaak Walton Hotel and Ilam Hall.

From the main car park cross the lane to a signposted track by the car park opposite. Follow the path over a double wooden stile between the two plantations ahead, then head left to the back of the Izaak Walton Hotel. Continue slightly left beyond the hotel as you start to rise up Bunster Hill, and aim for a stile in the wall ahead. Cross two stiles, then bear right towards the saddle of Bunster Hill and a wooden stile. Cross the stile and continue slightly right to a stone wall with steps in it. Turn left beyond the stile and follow the path over the saddle, rising as you go.

Once over the top of the saddle turn right and walk round the hillside, following the contours, before climbing again towards the obvious wall. Keep the wall to your left and continue rising to the brow of the hill.

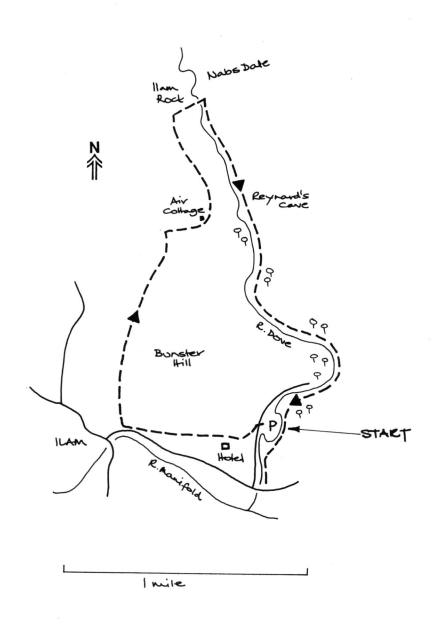

Here, a National Trust sign marks the start of their land, and lists various regulations to be adhered to when walking though Dovedale. Cross the stile, with the wall still to your left, and continue through a gate. Where the track joins another take a right turn and progress over the cattle grid to Air Cottage.

Take the track to the left, passing through the farm, and walk on to two gates. At a third gate take the stile to the right, folowed by a further stile on your right. Turn left here and follow the path through the superb mixed woodland to an old wall 400 yards on. Cross over the wall, a practice only to be taken where walls have collapsed to such an extent that climbing is unnecessary. Remember that drystone walls are difficult and expensive to replace. Left alone they can last for hundreds of years, but once people start climbing them they can soon degenerate to a pile of stones.

Follow the wire fence to where the wall resumes, running uphill, and take the descending path which winds down an old shooter's track to the river below. Ilam Rock is now to your right, and is reached by a somewhat muddy path running downstream along the west bank. At Ilam Rock take the footbridge across the river to Pickering Tor. You are now walking in the reverse direction to route 26 (Thorpe).

Pass Lion's Head Rock and the plaque to F.A. Holmes, and continue downstream. Along the way you will notice the intervention of man in the course of the Dove. Since the popularisation of the river by Walton and Cotton a great deal has been done to conserve the fish stocks of the river. The two main species found here are the brown trout and grayling. The grayling is a wholy freshwater member of the salmon family, closely related to the trout. It is easily identifiable by the long dorsal fin. In general it prefers fast flowing streams, but has prospered in the Dove despite the multitude of weirs.

Continue over the double stile and into The Narrows. Cross the boardwalk, looking up to your left to see Reynard's Cave and a huge natural arch. Pass the abandoned pumping station, with Dovedale Church opposite, and continue downstream. On the left are Tissington Spires, with Jacob's Ladder on the opposite bank, and a further double stile leads to the foot of Lovers' Leap.

Brown trout, one of the two main fish species in the Dove

Take the path over Sharplow Rise, with Dovedale Castle opposite, and follow the path as it bears right past the entrance to Lin Dale. Cross the Stepping Stones, if the water level allows, then turn left to the car park and your starting point. If you wish to check on the possibility of using the stepping stones prior to departure there is a water gauge to assess the river height.

28. LONGNOR

A short circular walk connecting the upper valleys of the Dove and Manifold, returning to Longnor.

Distance: 5 miles (8km)

Allow: 2 hours

Maps: White Peak 1:25000

How to get there

By car: Longnor lies south of Buxton and is accessible from the A515 Buxton to Ashbourne Road.

By train: no suitable stations nearby.

By bus: intermittent, seasonal services run between Longnor and Buxton.

Refreshments: there is a choice of pubs in Longnor.

From the car park at the centre of Longnor take the road leading out of the village to the east, signposted Crowdecote. Drop down from the ridge, keeping left as the road forks, and continue past the track to Gosslecroft (right). Take the next path on the right, shortly before an isolated building, and descend towards Bridge End Farm.

Cross the River Dove, then turn right as you approach the farm buildings. The path now heads south east along the ridge running from Crowdecote to Hartington. Keep on the main track, with the Dove below to your right, as you stay on a parallel course to the river across several fields. After a mile the river curves slightly to the right, but the path continues ahead. Below you to the right lie the remains of Pilsbury Castle, a Norman motte and bailey. As you approach the end of the castle embankment cross a wall and take the path to the right.

Keep the wall on your left hand side as you head towards the hamlet of Pilsbury. Turn right at the road and walk down into Pilsbury. As you

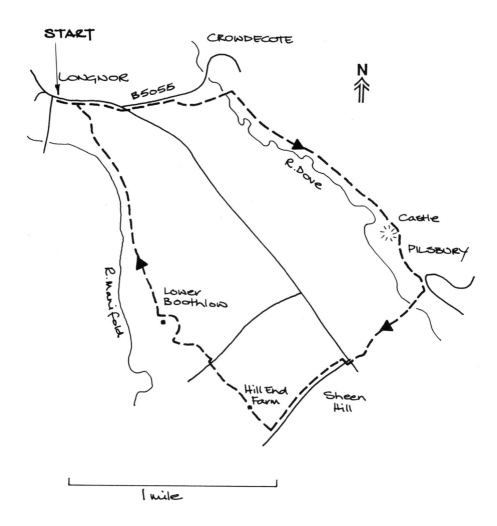

leave the hamlet a track leads off to your right, and down to a footbridge. Recross the Dove here and continue on, noting the ancient woodland to your right. The path now leads down to the Longnor – Hulme End road, and a right turn. Cross the road and turn left immediately down a further road. Continue rising as you pass to the right of Sheen Hill.

After half a mile take the track leading to your right, and walk through Hill End Farm. Stay on the left hand side of the wall as you descend slowly to a stream among trees. Cross the stream, a feeder of the Manifold, and pass to the right of the trees. The path now rises temporarily before dropping again to a road. Turn right at the road, then left, to descend again to a further feeder stream. Once over the stream follow the wall to your left as it curves round to Lower Boothlow Farm.

Beyond Lower Boothlow turn right to follow the path running parallel to the Manifold. Keep the wall to your right through the first field, then aim for the small square enclosure at the far end of the next field. Cross into the next field, and go straight ahead as a track crosses from left to right, with Upper Boothlow to your right. The path now gets progressively closer to the river as you move north towards Longnor. At this point the river valley is wide and flat, making ideal grazing land for the many farms.

Pass a track leading off right, then follow the path as it bears left round a bend in the river. As the river continues its curve the path straightens towards the wall ahead. Cross into the next field, then move diagonally left to join a further path leading left, and so back into Longnor.

29. HULME END

A gently ascending path round a less well used part of the Manifold Valley, starting and finishing at Hulme End.

Distance: 6 miles (9.5km)

Allow: 2 hours

Maps: White Peak 1:25000

How to get there

By car: Hulme End is most easily reached from Hartington. Take the A515 Buxton to Ashbourne road to the Hartington turn off (well signposted), then continue through the village in the direction of Warslow.

By train: no suitable stations nearby.

By bus: intermittent, seasonal services run between Longnor and Buxton.

Refreshments: the Manifold Valley Hotel at Hulme End.

Start from the car park on the west side of Hulme End on the B5054, Hartington Road. Turn left along the road, and continue to a path which exits right just after the farm. Bear diagonally to the left over the fields, with Hollow Farm to your right. Pass the farm via a stile in the hedge, then continue to a gate and wooden stile. The next gate is hidden in the wall, but cross the field moving slightly to your right to find it.

Cross the B5053, with Warslow Hall to the left, and move diagonally left as you cross a long narrow field. Pass Upper Brownhill Farm to your left and move slightly right to reach Steps Farm. Pass through the farm to a right turn at the far end of the yard, then cross the footbridge to pass Hayes Cottage. Take the stile beyond Hayes Cottage and bear left to the derelict Hayeshead. Walk across the front of the buildings to a gate at the top, then through a wet hollow which curves right to a track.

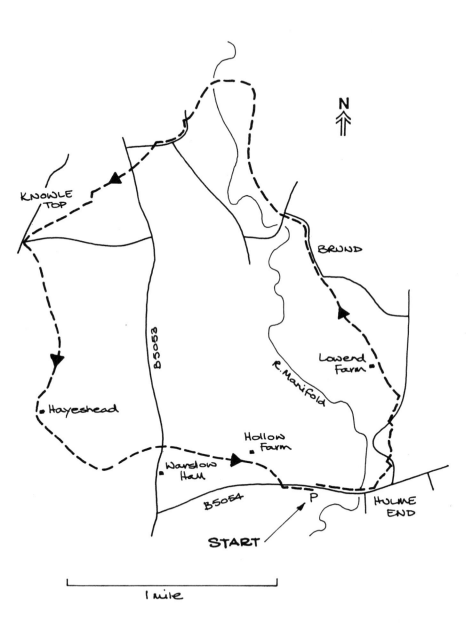

N

KNOWLE TOP

BRUND

B5053

Lowend Farm

R. Manifold

Hayeshead

Hollow Farm

Warslow Hall

B5054

P

HULME END

START

1 mile

Follow this track to a road where a right turn leads you to Knowle Top on your left. The road forks here, with the left hand branch leading to The Butchers Arms public house. The route onwards, however, heads directly on between the two forks and starts to drop. Keep left at the next fork, then left at a junction followed by a quick right turn between walls. Follow this track down to the A5053, and cross the road directly ahead.

Walk down this short section of path to emerge at a further road, with Marsh Farm ahead. Turn right along this road, then left at a junction. Cross a small stream then take the stile to your right. Turn slightly left and keep the field boundary to your right as you move down past Ludburn (left) to a bridge over the Manifold.

A gap in the hedge opposite leads to a path heading across the field to a stile and gate in the corner. Turn right, through the stile and drop down on the path to the riverside. As the river meanders to the right cross a stile and follow the fence to a wall stile on your left. Follow the track through the trees to a stile and a further short walk to the road. At the T-junction follow the uphill road which winds into Brund.

Walk through this hamlet along the road to a sharp left turn, then turn right over a stile. The path now descends to a bridge amongst the trees. Keep the wall to your left and follow the path down to a track, with a derelict farm on your right. Continue down the track to reach Lowend Farm, which you pass to your right, and on down to a road. Turn right down the road till a path exits left over a stile, then bear right to a stile in the left hand wall. Head across the gully to a stile in the hedge ahead, then turn slightly right to a further stile. Turn left along the road to a stile in the right hand wall, then aim for the stile to the left of the farm buildings. Turn right down this final section of road, cross the bridge and walk back into Hulme End and the car park.

30. ECTON

A circular route from Hulme End to Warslow via Ecton Hill and its historic copper mines, using a combination of the Manifold Track and quiet country lanes.

Distance: 2.5 miles (4km)

Allow: 1 hour

Maps: White Peak 1:25000

How to get there

By car: Hulme End is most easily reached from Hartington. Take the A515 Buxton to Ashbourne road to the Hartington turn off (well signposted), and continue through the village in the direction of Warslow.

By train: no suitable stations nearby.

By bus: intermittent, seasonal services run between Longnor and Buxton.

Refreshments: the Manifold Valley Hotel at Hulme End

Start from the car park on the west side of Hulme End on the B5054, Hartington Road. Take the ramp at the far end of the car park onto a path leading over a bridge. Continue onto the Manifold Track, another disused railway line converted for use by walkers and cyclists. Follow the track as it curves left along the floor of the river valley, with Westside Mill across the river to your left. As you approach the northern flanks of Ecton Hill the valley narrows considerably with tree-lined banks to either side climbing steeply. The track curves to the right, then left again, before crossing the Ecton road.

Ecton Hill on your left rises steeply to a height of 1200 ft, and is a unique feature in the Peak District. In the 18th century this was the site of the most productive copper mines in Europe, and the remains of many of these mines are still visible. While shafts and adits may appear inviting to the casual passerby, extreme caution should be taken here. Although closed for nearly two hundred years many of the passages provide sport to local cavers. Never drop stones down open shafts as there may be someone below, and adits should only be entered when wearing correct equipment and in the company of an experienced guide.

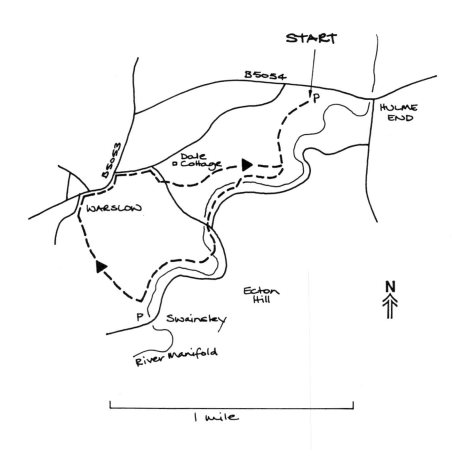

Continue along the track to a gateway and small car park at Swainsley. Beyond the gate take a footpath leading uphill to the right to a short ramp and a stile. Turn half-right at the stile to progress up a gully. Pass the remains of a series of steps and a stile to reach a further stile. Cross this stile through a hedge, and turn right to follow the hedgerow to another stile. Continue uphill, passing a derelict building to your left, and over two stiles. Further uphill are a gate and stile; beyond these follow the path up to a lane. Turn right at the lane, and then right again to the village of Warslow.

Walk through Warslow to a lane leading off left beyond Hobcroft Farm. Take the first turning to the right, before Dale Cottage, and continue to a right hand bend. At the crown of the bend turn right and, keeping the wall to your left, head downhill above the north bank of the river. The wooded slopes dropping away to your left are those you passed on the way round to Swainsley, and across the river is Ecton Hill. At the far end of the trees you meet the Manifold Track, but cross onto the path runnning straight ahead.

The path now heads half-right to the river, then turns half-left across the valley before ascending to the Manifold Track again. Continue ahead to rejoin the lane from Warslow via two consecutive right turns, then pass Cowlow to emerge once more at Upper Hulme.

31. WETTON

A circular route around the River Manifold from Wetton Mill, taking in Wetton Mill, Thor's Cave and Bincliffe lead mines.

Distance: 7 miles (11 km)

Allow: 3 hours

Maps: White Peak 1:25000

How to get there

By car: Wetton Mill and Wetton are located east of Alstonefield in the Manifold Valley, and easily reached from the A515 Buxton to Ashbourne road

By train: no suitable stations nearby.

By bus: intermittent, seasonal services run from Buxton.

Refreshments: Royal Oak at Wetton

From Wetton Mill take the path which leads north-east through the obvious valley. Walk up the dale, with Wetton Hill to your right and steep slopes to either side. Continue alongside the stream to a stile at the head of the dale, then take a further stile opposite Manor House Farm. Turn right here down to a footbridge, then take the right hand path ahead.

The path now clings to a wall on your right as it takes the easiest course between two hills.

Keep close to the wall as the path bends right, and continue to the stile in the corner. Continue straight on as the path cuts across the next field, then over the following stile. Pass to the left of some isolated rocks, and continue down to pass an old quarry and reservoir. The path now drops into Wetton village, passing the Royal Oak.

Continue through Wetton village and take the road towards Alstonfield. Just prior to the second road on the left, a stile on your right leads into

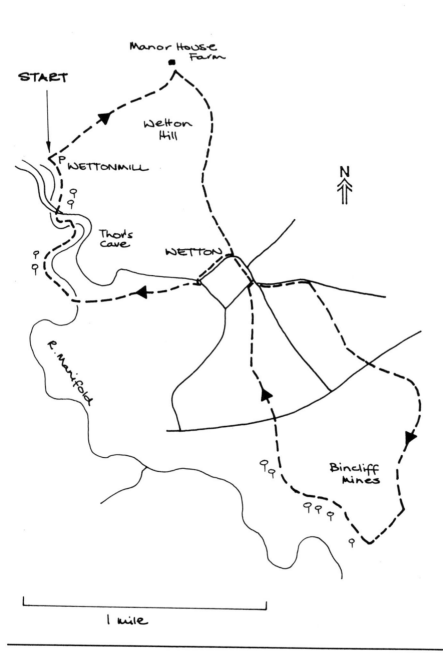

the fields. The path continues ahead, through a series of stiles before bearing left to a road. Cross the road and the stile opposite and continue bearing right across the fields. At the crossroads of paths, take a right turn and keep the wall to your right as you descend to a lane.

Cross the lane and continue your descent towards the woods ahead. At the next junction, turn right and walk along the edge of the woods with a wall on your right.

Pass the last few shafts of the former Bincliffe Mine, which has an adit deep in the woods below, and continue past a lane leading off right. The path cuts through the far end of the woods temporarily before emerging close to a road. Cross the road, and then go straight across the next road onto a path, with the wall to your left. Keep the wall to the left as you carry on to a T-junction. Turn right at the junction and follow the path across the fields into Wetton village again.

From Wetton follow the lane towards Wetton Mill to a signposted track leading up to Thor's Cave, just after a gate and farm track. Continue up the steep-sided valley, across a stile, and onwards to a gate. As you walk through the thick vegetation a path leads up to the left for those wishing to see the cave. From here the main path continues downhill towards the river. At the end of the path turn right onto the Manifold Track. This soon leads to a road junction, where a left turn leads back to your starting point at Wetton Mill.

32. ALSTONEFIELD

A long route linking the Manifold and Dove valleys, and taking in the villages of Ilam, Wetton and Alstonefield.

Distance: 11 miles (17.5km)

Allow: 4 hours

Maps: White Peak 1:25000

How to get there

By car: the village of Ilam is reached by a continuation of the Thorpe road from the A515.

By train: no suitable stations nearby.

By bus: intermittent, seasonal services run from Buxton.

Refreshments: There are a café and hotel at Ilam, the Royal Oak at Wetton and a pub at Alstonefield.

Ilam is located near the confluence of the Manifold and Dove, and over the years has become an important tourist centre. The village itself has a number of points of interest, including the Gothic cross, Izaak Walton Hotel and Ilam Hall. The Ilam Hall complex includes gardens, camping and caravan site, information centre, café and youth hostel, and is an important attraction to the area. In recent years a lot of work has been carried out around Bunster Hill, with trees being planted and a car park and toilet block being extended for the benefit of walkers.

Walk south from the village to the banks of the Manifold and take the path which runs up the east side of the river. At this point the river valley is at its widest and flattest, making a superb contrast to the steep wooded slopes opposite. Continue upstream as the river curves right, through a giant meander, along tree-lined banks to a footbridge. Cross the river and continue across the fields ahead, ignoring the bridge to

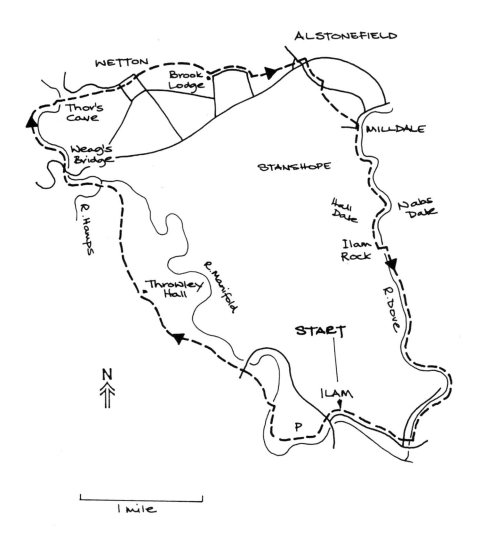

your left. Pass Rushley Farm to your left, then take the farm track to the left. To your left lies a beautiful wooded valley which winds through ash and alder to the village of Calton, but your route lies onwards along the track that contours to Throwley Hall. Continue through the farm, and immediately through the second gate to a stile on the right.

Bear slightly right through the next field, then more sharply right as you aim for the gap between two narrow belts of trees. Pass the main line of trees to your left and, ignoring the path entering from your left, continue down the hill. The path now drops to the river valley where the Hamps meets the Manifold. In dry weather both river courses may be dry, as the rivers run underground to emerge downstream near Ilam.

Cross the Hamps and continue along the disused line of the Manifold Track (formerly the Manifold Valley Light Railway). Progress along the track, with the Manifold below to your right, to Weags Bridge and Ladyside. High on the right is the opening to Thor's Cave, and shortly after is a path leading to a bridge across the river. Climb steeply through the trees, then through the last few fields into Wetton.

Walk through Wetton, turning right, then left, to pass the church. Cross a stile in front and walk down to to the valley bottom via several stiles. At the valley bottom turn right along a wide track to a road.

Turn left by Brook Lodge, along the road, and take the third stile on the left to ascend into Alstonefield. Walk through the village, turning right down the road to Milldale, to a footpath on the right. Continue through the fields to emerge at the hamlet of Milldale, and Dovedale.

Follow the path alongside the river through National Trust land. The river and path meander through the valley between Stanshope Pasture (right) and Baley Hill (left). Pass below the crags of Ravens Tor, another popular name throughout the peak, and on to the junctions of Nabs Dale and Hall Dale with Dovedale. Ilam Rock is now to your right, and is reached by a somewhat muddy path running downstream along the west bank. At Ilam Rock take the footbridge across the river to Pickering Tor. You are now walking the reverse direction to route 26 (Thorpe).

Pass Lion's Head Rock and the plaque to F.A. Holmes, and continue downstream. Continue over the double stile and into The Narrows.

Reynard's Cave (by permission, Peak National Park)

Cross the boardwalk, looking up to your left to see Reynard's Cave and a huge natural arch.

Pass the abandoned pumping station, with Dovedale Church opposite, and continue downstream. On the left are Tissington Spires, with Jacob's Ladder on the opposite bank, and a further double stile leads to the foot of Lovers' Leap.

Take the path over Sharplow Rise, with Dovedale Castle opposite, and follow the path as it bears right past the entrance to Lin Dale. Continue down beside the river to emerge at the road by St. Mary's Bridge. From here a short walk leads back up the road to Ilam, and welcome refreshments.